Praise for *Playing with FIRE*

"In *Playing with FIRE*, Scott Rieckens shares the essence of the FIRE movement. And he does it with deeply personal, honest, and captivating stories that keep the pages turning. If you're at all interested in financial independence, retiring early, or just putting happiness ahead of money, you will enjoy this book."

— **Chad Carson**, creator of the blog *Coach Carson* and author of *Retire Early with Real Estate*

"Scott Rieckens has done a phenomenal job of embracing the FIRE movement and making the hard choices necessary to radically alter his family's financial future. His book should be an inspiration to anyone starting in a similar life position. If you feel stuck or feel that you are not able to flex your creative talents and live a life where you are in control, then *Playing with FIRE* might be just the book you need."

— **Scott Trench**, author of *Set for Life* and host of the *BiggerPockets Money* podcast

"This is a fascinating, relatable, and heartfelt story about a couple's transition from ultra-consumers to people who discovered that time is more valuable than belongings. It weaves together their personal journey with actionable information, and features examples of dozens of others who are leaving the rat race in search of meaning. You won't be able to put this book down."

— **Paula Pant**, founder of affordanything.com

"A truly inspirational story that proves saving is not a sacrifice. It's a path to a life you love."

— **Grant Sabatier**, author of *Financial Freedom* and creator of millennialmoney.com

"With the enthusiasm of a convert and a filmmaker's feel for story-telling, Scott recounts his own and others' journeys in pursuit of FIRE so that readers can try it on for themselves to see if it fits.

You'll love meeting the bloggers and writers who've stoked the 'fire' and the ordinary people who've been transformed by it."

— **Vicki Robin,** coauthor of *Your Money or Your Life* and author of *Blessing the Hands That Feed Us*

"The path to FIRE is not linear, and this book perfectly captures the ups and downs many people face along the way. It's rare, however, to get such an intimate view into a family's journey from the very beginning. This book gives you that and is a fantastic behind-the-scenes look at the upcoming documentary. It contains interesting backstory, endearing personal moments, and actionable advice to help you achieve your own financial goals sooner."

— **Brandon Ganch,** *Mad Fientist*

"What if you could change your life 180 degrees, break free of the paycheck-to-paycheck grind, and pursue financial independence? Scott and Taylor Rieckens chronicle their incredible turnaround in *Playing with FIRE*, and their brilliantly simple advice is applicable to anyone: Spend less than you earn, invest the difference, and create the space in your life to pursue true happiness and lifelong relationships."

— **Brad Barrett** and **Jonathan Mendonsa,** cohosts of the *ChooseFI* podcast

"To the uninitiated, pursuing financial independence seems exotic, impossible, and/or daunting. But in fact, it is simple and has roots deep in the American psyche. If you wonder what this path is like in real life and in real time, Scott and Taylor will take you along on their journey: not yet finished, a work in progress, and a very engaging tale."

— **JL Collins,** author of *The Simple Path to Wealth*

PLAYING WITH

FIRE

FINANCIAL
INDEPENDENCE
RETIRE EARLY

PLAYING WITH FIRE

FIRE

FINANCIAL
INDEPENDENCE
RETIRE EARLY

HOW FAR WOULD YOU GO
FOR FINANCIAL FREEDOM?

SCOTT RIECKENS

New World Library
Novato, California

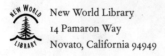

New World Library
14 Pamaron Way
Novato, California 94949

Text design by Tona Pearce Myers and Rodrigo Calderon

Library of Congress Cataloging-in-Publication Data
Names: Rieckens, Scott, date, author.
Title: Playing with fire (financial independence retire early) : how far would you
    go for financial freedom? / Scott Rieckens.
Description: Novato, California : New World Library, [2019] | Includes index.
Identifiers: LCCN 2018047667 (print) | LCCN 2018049920 (ebook) | ISBN
    9781608685813 (e-book) | ISBN 9781608685806 (print : alk. paper) | ISBN
    9781608685813 (Ebook)
Subjects: LCSH: Early retirement. | Thriftiness. | Finance, Personal.
Classification: LCC HD7110 (ebook) | LCC HD7110 .R54 2019 (print) | DDC
    332.024/014--dc23
LC record available at https://lccn.loc.gov/2018047667

First printing, January 2019
ISBN 978-1-60868-580-6
Ebook ISBN 978-1-60868-581-3

Printed in Canada on 100% postconsumer-waste recycled paper

New World Library is proud to be a Gold Certified Environmentally Responsible Publisher. Publisher certification awarded by Green Press Initiative. www.greenpressinitiative.org

10   9   8   7   6   5   4   3   2   1

CONTENTS

FOREWORD

Modern life is more prosperous and fancy than it has ever been. The cars are faster, TVs are bigger, and food is cheaper (in proportion to the average income) than it has been for most of world history. So why does it seem so difficult to make ends meet?

The reason is that there's a huge, well-engineered, brilliantly marketed trap sitting between us and our real goal of living the happy and fulfilling lives we want, and it ensnares us into the busy, expensive, stressed, confusing existence almost all of us are leading these days. The trap is sometimes called "consumerism," but it is so universal and well disguised that most people just refer to it as "reality."

So in rich countries like the United States, almost all of us live our lives from within the jaws of this trap. We trade most of our free time for money by working the highest-paying job we can find, but then we trade most of this money for the most expensive stuff we can possibly afford, in most cases even borrowing or leasing this stuff so we can claw our way even higher up the luxury scale whenever we get the chance.

In the likely event of a money shortage, we assume we just need to go out and earn even more of it. And when this causes an even worse shortage of time, we just strap in tighter and reward ourselves with a few of the finer things in life — because if we're going to work *this hard*, we should at least get to see some of the rewards.

Stop it. It's a trap — all of it!

But how can you stop, when the entire world around you is

caught in the same trap and may even question or criticize you if you choose not to do the same thing as they are doing? What if your spouse refuses to give up his comfortable, roomy SUV or her well-curated wardrobe of professional clothing, even if it means spending most of your lifetime in debt?

The trap has been laid out for us with over a century of clever marketing, but its biggest strength is our built-in human weakness: our tendency to compare ourselves to those around us and assume that whatever we see in our peers is *normal and worth emulating.*

And it is absolutely *not* worth emulating. In fact, it's a proven recipe for failure, which is why the average forty-year-old American has only a few thousand dollars to their name, after almost twenty years of work. Obtaining money and freedom is just like any other skill in life: in order to be more *successful* than your peers, you need to do things *differently* than they do.

I happened to be born frugal — with a desire to get the most fun out of my own money while having no natural instinct to follow what other people were doing with theirs. And I also happened to go through my early financial life with a partner who felt the same way. So there was not much resistance on our short career path to retiring around age thirty.

But most people face a much more difficult journey. They may have started life with higher spending and debt, and grown into a life with a more vibrant culture of spending all around them. And they may have married someone who was on that same program. Once you get locked into a lifestyle like this, it can be very tricky to climb back out of it.

That's why this book about Scott and Taylor's story is so meaningful to me. They have been able to share their *journey* across a gigantic chasm of life perspective. They ran into hardships that I think a lot of people will relate to, and even more amazingly, they *overcame* each of these hardships, kept going, and found ways to renegotiate their differences while keeping their marriage strong and their friendships intact.

They have come out the other side of it all with a decades-shorter jail sentence of mandatory work, even as their energy for working on projects that make a difference is higher than ever. To put it frankly, I never would have imagined this could happen for a family like the one Scott describes at the beginning of the story.

But having seen their success, I now have even higher hopes that more people can reap the benefits of more financially independent lives everywhere. And I think you will feel that same hope creep into your *own* outlook on life as you read it.

— **Pete Adeney a.k.a. Mr. Money Mustache**

INTRODUCTION TO FIRE

The quest for a happy and meaningful life is not new. Socrates tells us that the secret to happiness is found not in seeking more but in developing the capacity to be happy with less. Confucius states that the more a person "meditates upon good thoughts," the happier he or she will be. Aristotle says that "happiness depends upon ourselves," not on the kind of watch we wear or the number of countries we've visited. Even modern research shows that, to quote one study, "close relationships, more than money or fame, are what keep people happy throughout their lives." None of this is news, I'm sure. If I said, "Having a nice house won't make you happy," you would most likely nod and agree without hesitation. And yet many of us remain stuck in a cycle of overworking and overspending, reaching for instant gratification instead of seeking deeper and more durable satisfaction. I have been guilty of this, too: My wife, Taylor, and I sacrificed peace of mind, time together, time with our child, and meaningful relationships in order to work harder and harder so we could pay for more and more. We knew better than to think fancy cars and nice dinners would equal happiness, but that sure didn't stop us from trying.

Then, at age thirty-three, I was introduced to a fascinating phenomenon known as FIRE, which stands for "financial independence retire early." FIRE is a growing community of people of all types and income levels committed to lives of aggressive savings and low-cost investments in order to take control of their finances and buy back their most precious resource, time. The end goal is to achieve "FIRE," the state of having enough passive income that you don't need to work to pay your living expenses. Many people who reach FIRE keep working out of their passion for their fields, but plenty of others quit to travel the world, start nonprofits, pursue creative projects, or just *live simply*. In fact, despite the term "retire early" in the movement's name, I've found the people in the FIRE community often reject the word *retire* and its implications; financial independence is about having the freedom and flexibility to pursue your true calling, whether or not it makes any money. FIRE isn't about drinking cocktails on a beach for the rest of your life. It's about spending your precious years on earth doing something other than sitting behind a desk, counting the minutes to 5 PM, wishing you were somewhere else.

In the process of writing this book, I came to see FIRE as the antidote to the "daily grind" of employment. Maybe you love your job. Maybe you don't — in which case, you're not alone: Half of Americans aren't satisfied at their jobs. Regardless of how you feel about your job, you probably feel that you have no choice but to keep working (I know that's how I felt). On the other hand, if you were financially independent, you could quit at any time. Even if your job is fulfilling, you probably wouldn't mind the freedom to move on if and when you wanted to. If you depend on your paycheck, you are likely compromising on some aspect of your life, and quitting your job would mean facing financial uncertainty. But what if you didn't depend on a paycheck? What would you choose to do then? FIRE, ultimately, offers that freedom.

Sounds pretty good, right? So how do you achieve this carefree life? Well, you spend less, save more, and invest the difference. The general path to FIRE is to save 50 to 70 percent of your income, invest those savings in low-fee stock index funds, and retire in roughly ten years. Of course, the actual numbers differ for everyone, but I've provided the key equations and FIRE formulas throughout the book, and you can plug your numbers into these to determine whether FIRE is the right path for you.

Ultimately, "spending less" is the critical, most-difficult part of this equation, and the creative, quirky, and ingenious lifestyle hacks that the FIRE community has developed are impressive, even if I have no intention of implementing each and every tactic in my own life. That's because FIRE is flexible. You get to try it on; shop before you buy, if you will. Common FIRE practices include living with roommates or moving to a cheaper area, cooking all meals at home, buying used cars with cash, going to a one- or zero-car household, buying groceries in bulk, embracing budget or "hacked" travel, and giving up luxury purchases like fancy purses, shoes, watches, electronics, jewelry, and furniture. More extreme FIRE practitioners might live out of an RV or trailer home, grow their own food, stop shopping entirely for years at a time, bike to work in subzero temperatures, or even leave the country in search of a lower-cost lifestyle.

When I discovered FIRE in early 2017, I was certainly not making choices like these. I wouldn't have blinked at spending $300 on a dinner, flying off to Vegas for a weekend golf trip with my buds, or leasing a brand-new car. It's an understatement to say that I was fascinated by the people making these extreme lifestyle choices. What kind of commitment does that take? What does it feel like to give up the "normal" trappings of a middle-class life? And if I had access to so many more luxuries and experiences than these people did in my everyday life, why wasn't I happier? Or better yet, why did they seem so happy?

HOW MUCH MONEY DOES IT TAKE TO BE HAPPY?

According to research published in *Nature*, there is an optimal point for the level of income it takes to make an individual happy. After surveying more than 1.7 million people in 164 countries, the researchers concluded that the ideal income for emotional well-being is $60,000 to $75,000 (or the local currency equivalent). That means earning more than $75,000 may make you momentarily happy, but it won't actually increase your life satisfaction in any meaningful way.

As my excitement about the FIRE movement grew, I was also intrigued by my internal response to it and the emotional impact it seemed to have on others. Supporters referred to it as "life-changing" and "the key to happiness," while naysayers scoffed at the idea that a frugal life could feel bountiful, and they pointed out that retiring in your forties was guaranteed to be boring. As someone who always felt like my job was the thing funding my creative endeavors, boredom didn't concern me. The frugal part, on the other hand, terrified me. At the time, Taylor and I considered our lifestyle pretty average, though today I consider it extravagant. The idea of cutting our expenses in half seemed impossible. We led a six-figure lifestyle, which was hard to give up, especially when most of that *felt* like it was going to "needs" instead of "wants." As we adopted FIRE, we struggled, we fought, we made mistakes, and occasionally, we talked about throwing in the towel and just going back to our old spending habits.

But after a couple of months of drastically cutting our

expenses, I was inspired by the transformational effects of living a simpler, lower-cost lifestyle. Not only did I want to continue learning FIRE tactics and philosophies, but I wanted to learn more about the FIRE community and how this idea is changing lives around the world. Since I had spent the previous decade working as a film director and producer, it dawned on me that writing a book and creating a FIRE documentary could be a great opportunity to immerse myself in this new way of life. I would use platforms that I know well to learn everything I could about something I didn't know at all. These efforts would be a vehicle for me and Taylor to hold ourselves accountable to this new lifestyle by documenting both the mechanics of FIRE and how we were embracing its principles in our lives. From this, *Playing with FIRE* was born, and you are holding one of the results, this book, in your hands. The documentary is due to be released in 2019. Both projects share our story long before I know how it will turn out. Will we fail? Has this been a mistake? A flop? At this point, all I know is that the concept of FIRE has improved my life, and I want to share it with as many people as possible in hopes that it will improve their lives as well.

IS FIRE ONLY FOR RICH PEOPLE?

Over the past year, I've been asked this question again and again: *Is FIRE only for rich people?*

That's a bit of a loaded question, and all I can share is my experience. I've connected with thousands of people who are pursuing FIRE, and I've been contacted by thousands more. What I've seen is that for every engineer making $200,000, I've also met a family on a yearly combined income of $70,000.

I've talked to single people and to families with four and five kids. I've met baristas making $35,000 and stockbrokers making $400,000. People who haven't graduated high school and people with PhDs. People who live in big cities like New York and LA, who live in rural counties in Kentucky and Iowa, and who live in foreign countries like Indonesia, France, Sweden, Ireland, and Mexico.

That isn't to say that there's not some validity in the question: FIRE is significantly easier to accomplish if you're making a higher-than-average salary. For most millennials, especially those who graduated college during the 2008 recession with record high levels of student debt, the idea of amassing large amounts of wealth feels ridiculously out of reach. But FIRE principles can be applied at any income level. Whether you reach FIRE in five, ten, or thirty years, the benefits of spending less and saving more, prioritizing happiness over material objects, and buying back your time are available to everyone. Whatever you have, whoever you are, whatever you earn, you deserve peace of mind, and FIRE is a pathway. Throughout the book, I've included FIRE stories that highlight people from every kind of background and economic opportunity who are pursuing FIRE. I hope you'll find inspiration hearing from others in a similar situation.

If your first impulse, as mine was, is to disregard FIRE as a bunch of penny-pinching weirdos who live in tiny homes, let me give you a snapshot of the alternative: In 2017, consumer debt hit a record high at nearly $13 trillion. At the same time, household savings hit a twelve-year low. A 2016 survey reported that 69 percent of Americans have less than $1,000 in savings, and 34 percent have no savings at all. Nobody should have to live under financial stress, and yet many of us do. I did, and our financial situation was significantly better than most:

In 2016, Taylor and I made $186,000 ($142,000 after taxes), and we had just paid off the last of our combined student loans of $35,000 the year before. Still, despite our higher-than-average salaries, Taylor and I were spending almost every penny we made.

If you're like most people, your income, net worth, and level of debt aren't things you openly discuss. A few years ago, a Wells Fargo survey found that money ranked as the number one most-difficult topic to talk about. Amazingly, death, religion, and politics all ranked beneath money. Until I joined the FIRE community, I had numerous close friends and family members with whom I could share almost anything, but I would never have discussed my paycheck or how much was in my 401k. Why? My theory is that discussing money is challenging because of all that it represents: success, meaning, power, status. Money is a shorthand for so many other things.

The FIRE community couldn't be more different. From online forums to in-person meetups to bloggers posting monthly updates about their net worth — the FIRE community is built on the principles of openness and collaboration. And as I have become more and more immersed in the FIRE community, I've come to see that secrecy around money harms much more than it helps. What are we trying to hide? Guilt? Shame? Fear? Is that fear originating from our upbringing? Are we afraid of being seen as greedy or as foolish? On the other hand, when we share information and knowledge freely, everyone benefits. That's why, while writing this book, Taylor and I decided to be completely transparent about our finances: about how much we make, how much we spend and save, and how FIRE has affected us. We want to do our part to make money part of everyday conversation. Not to make our example the benchmark, not as a form of comparison. Rather, to release the power money has over us. To help *you* reshape your relationship with money and what it really means to you. Money is a means to an end. And your means and your end are up to you. As you read this book, even if you aren't comfortable sharing your financial details with your loved ones, consider joining an online forum where you can talk about money honestly and openly (and anonymously, if you prefer).

Everyone's story is different, and I'm aware that the financial position Taylor and I were in when we started FIRE may not reflect yours. Neither of us grew up in affluent families, but we were both incredibly lucky to attend college, leave school with minimal student debt, and in the years afterward, avoid credit card debt. We have been blessed with good health and haven't had to deal with any kind of financial crisis or emergency that would put us deeper into debt or limit our earnings. We are lucky to have developed skills and harnessed opportunities in industries that pay well. That said, in one significant way, our story reflects an extremely common problem: Rather than make the most of what we had, we were squandering it. Instead of maximizing our opportunities, or giving back to the world, Taylor and I were spending our lives working as much as possible so that we could slowly check off a long list of purchases that we thought would make us feel happy and important. What a waste! Like many people, as we earned more, we experienced "lifestyle creep": the tendency to buy nicer things, eat out more, and play more expensively. Indeed, we often don't notice all the ways our expenses rise to meet our income, and when lifestyle creep is left unchecked, it can be dangerous, even lethal, to financial health over the long term.

My goal with *Playing with FIRE* is to offer an intimate view of an alternate path — a unique and interesting life design and philosophy that definitely bucks the trend. I'm a firm believer in "to each their own," and clearly, this path is not for everyone. But I hope my story will inspire you to take a deeper look at your own financial and lifestyle choices. Are you trading your time for dollars? What kind of legacy do you want to leave behind? If this book, its message, and the examples in it can help even a few people live a happier and more financially secure life, then I'll consider this effort a smashing success.

The story you're about to read is my family's journey from overspending to saving half of our income, from a luxurious life living by the beach to traveling around the country hunting for a new (and less-expensive) place to live. As I've written this book, I've tried to be as candid as possible. I've made sure to include not just our successes, but our failures and struggles as well as actual dollar amounts. I've also asked Taylor to add her perspective throughout the book. My goal is to show you the real journey of a family pursuing FIRE, and I hope that it inspires you to seek your own version of freedom.

CHAPTER 1

WORK,
EAT,
SLEEP,
REPEAT

If you'd driven by me on the freeway in San Diego on this particular Monday morning in February 2017, you probably wouldn't have looked twice: a guy in his midthirties sitting in traffic in a relatively new but unremarkable car, drinking a cold brew from Starbucks. Just another American heading to work.

In fact, there was nothing particularly special about that Monday morning, and I would have lumped it in with a hundred other ordinary Monday mornings that I had spent navigating traffic on my way to work, except that on this particular morning I heard an idea that would change the course of my entire life. An idea that would cause me to quit my job, leave California, and spend a year traveling with my family. To question everything I thought I knew about success, money, and freedom. To find the secret to the American dream, the thing that most people crave but few achieve: the ability to do absolutely anything I wanted.

■ ■ ■ ■

This story starts ten years earlier, when I met my wife, Taylor.

From the beginning, Taylor and I were the couple who sought adventure and wanted to live large. New Year's in Vegas? Sure. Last-minute spa trip to Sonoma? Why not! We weren't spending money on flashy watches or designer clothes — but boating on Lake Tahoe? Four-star restaurants? A new snowboard? Flights around the world? Absolutely. We developed an interest in fancy wine and an expensive restaurant habit. When a new restaurant opened, we made sure to try it. If we could meet the chef, even better. Sometimes we ate out three or four times a week.

We joked that our motto was "If we have the money in the bank, go for it." And we did: As hard as we worked to earn money, it all went right back out the door to pay for our good times. That was fine by us. As long as we didn't go into debt, we felt like we were doing life right. Certainly, at times, I would stress about how much money we were spending or how little savings we had. Then I would remind myself that we were young — there was so much time to save in the future! We would hit some big payday, land some huge job, or perhaps sell a business for millions. Eventually, something would surely get us there! Right? We habitually used this "lottery mentality" to feel better about our lack of control.

At the time, I was managing events for one of the largest beer corporations in the world. My job consisted of being flown around the West Coast to support events like the NBA and MLB All-Star games, the Sundance Film Festival, music festivals, and so on. For me, a restless kid who loves adventure and meeting new people, it felt like a dream job. But after a year on the road, the parties and events began to blend together. I started to question the long-term viability of this line of work. I could feel myself craving something more creative and meaningful. I was traveling constantly, barely sleeping, and living an unhealthy lifestyle. I knew I could not keep this up for long. I wanted a life of outdoor adventure, physical activity, and connection. Something that felt more exciting than drinking beer and missing out on quality time with my family.

■ ■ ■ ■

After Taylor and I married in 2010, we honeymooned in the island nation of St. Kitts and Nevis. On the flight back, Taylor leaned her head against the airplane seat and said, "Why can't we just live somewhere every day that feels like a vacation?" We were currently living in Reno but we were both ready for a change of scenery. Ten minutes later, we had made a list of "paradise" locales on the back of a drink napkin: St. John in the US Virgin Islands, Kauai, Coronado, Scottsdale, and Key West. After some back-and-forth, in early 2012, we packed up our house in Reno, quit our jobs, and moved to Coronado, California, outside San Diego, hoping to find our endless vacation. We wanted a life that felt enjoyable every day instead of just living for the weekend. We told ourselves we wouldn't be like other people who talk about moving to the beach but never follow through. In retrospect, this atypical move was great training for our FIRE lifestyle to come, but it was also part of our problem.

For the first few years, living in Coronado really did feel like living in paradise. We rented a little one-bedroom apartment near the bay and would stroll the boardwalk to watch the sunset reflect off the beautiful downtown skyline. We bought two beach cruisers and biked everywhere — to the beach, around the city, to meet our friends for drinks after work. It felt like we had the life that everyone dreams of: carefree, outdoorsy, relaxed.

As our love of the outdoors grew, so did our collection of outdoor gear. We bought kayaks, stand-up paddleboards, and surfboards. Then we needed a fleet to carry all our gear, so we bought a Chevy Equinox SUV and a Toyota Prius, complete with sunroofs and roof racks, because — California.

We found loads of career opportunities in San Diego, a city on the rise. Taylor worked for her family's recruiting company and steadily built her market and network. I co-owned a video production company that was eventually acquired, and we moved into a larger marketing agency's office. The cultures didn't quite mesh, and eventually my partners and I decided to move on and start fresh. Doing this meant leaving a large amount of money on the table, but I felt it was the right decision. I have always prioritized my freedom over a paycheck, and I knew that I had the potential to build another successful business. I had developed the skills; I just needed to give myself a chance.

Then we decided to have a baby.

■ ■ ■ ■

Our daughter was born in October 2015. It was a perfect California day: sunny, with clear skies and an ocean breeze. We named her Jovie, a reference to the word *jovial*, because we wanted her to chase joy in her life the same way we were.

Like most first-time parents, we had gone above and beyond in getting ready for Jovie's arrival. We'd moved out of the one-bedroom rental apartment and into a tiny but more accommodating three-bedroom house. Taylor was working from home at this point, and she wanted her own office. Plus, we knew family members would visit to see Jovie, so we wanted a guest bedroom. After weeks of searching, we found a rental house for $2,850 a month, which was a steal in Coronado. We promptly spent another $8,000 furnishing our new home, along with stocking a new nursery with a crib and all the amenities. No cost was spared as we prepared for our new baby.

By this point in our lives, we had recently spent $6,000 to become boat club members, and we were leasing two cars — a 2016 Mazda 3 Hatchback and a 2015 BMW 3 Series GT.

Before Jovie was born, Taylor and I could both feel that our expenses were getting out of hand. We occasionally talked about cutting back. But whenever we tried, we ended up convincing ourselves we just *had* to have whatever it was that we wanted, like a Vitamix blender, a vacation to New Zealand, or the best Italian-made stroller for our little coconut. We had the money, and we both innocently assumed that it would all work out, that our incomes would keep increasing and we'd eventually start saving for the future.

After all, Taylor's salary was good, and my new company was already making a profit. Plus, we were being financially responsible by contributing to our 401k retirement accounts (usually around 10 percent of our income). That said, aside from our retirement accounts, neither of us were invested in the stock market. We were unfamiliar with investing, stocks felt too risky, and our busy schedules were always a convenient excuse for why we didn't have time to learn more. Besides, everything looked good: We had high-paying jobs; we were contributing to our 401ks; and we had avoided consumer debt. Surely, we were on the right path.

Then Jovie arrived, and Taylor had an epiphany that many parents experience: Within weeks, she couldn't bear the thought of having to work again and be separated from her infant daughter for eight hours a day. Taylor enjoyed her work, and she'd never considered being a stay-at-home mom. Now, given our financial situation, she had no choice. When her abbreviated maternity leave ended, Taylor went back to full-time work, and we hired a nanny to watch Jovie during the day, which cost $2,500 a month. Neither of us wanted Taylor to have to work, but it was our only option: We needed two incomes to afford our lifestyle.

As the months passed, Taylor became increasingly distraught as she thought about all the moments with her baby that she was missing. It killed me to see her feeling this way, and the worst part was that I felt responsible. Why hadn't I pushed us to save more money before we'd decided to have a child? Had I made a mistake by leaving that larger agency, and its higher income, so I could start my own business? Taylor had supported this decision, even though it meant more financial instability, as well as travel and long workdays. Now I wondered if she regretted it. Did she feel like my entrepreneurial dreams were standing in the way of her happiness? Was she giving up time with our child so I could pursue my personal ambition? And while all this was swirling, I found myself getting more stressed-out thinking how little time I'd have with Jovie if I took on all this myself. Holy moly, was there a right answer out there? Why was this so hard?

Then one of my partners decided to leave our production company, and the business fell apart. We had started four years ago when we were a bunch of young guys in our twenties, full of optimism and energy for our work. And we were successful: We turned our company from a small wedding-video outfit into a desirable commercial-video production company with seven-figure revenues. Of course, we worked our asses off to do it; the job was a grind. At first, this sacrifice was manageable, but now our lives looked completely different: We had kids, families, mortgages, daycare costs. We couldn't travel for weeks at a time anymore. We longed for company-sponsored health insurance and 401ks. We wanted stability, not this feast-or-famine lifestyle. When that partner decided to leave, we collectively decided it was time to move on.

Within a month, we shuttered our agency, and once again I was untethered, searching for my next opportunity. Selfishly, I wanted to start a media company, creating content that interested me. But we couldn't afford for me to start over again; our lifestyle required two full-time earners. So I accepted a job as a creative director at a promising young creative agency called Grizzly. The team was loaded with talent, and I was excited to learn more about brand design, strategy, and development. It was a great job with a stable paycheck, but it still didn't solve our problem: our lifestyle. Even with this job, we were never going to get ahead. And did this mean I would be locked in a salaried job indefinitely, with no chance to pursue entrepreneurship?

At the same time that I became a salaried worker, costs

that had always seemed far off were starting to seem alarmingly close. Like buying a house. The equivalent of our small three-bedroom rental would cost over a million to buy in Coronado, and $600,000 to $750,000 anywhere else in San Diego. And what about college? Weren't new parents supposed to save for that? Beyond contributing to our retirement funds, we didn't have any extra savings. The choices that had once felt carefree and spontaneous now felt foolhardy and reckless.

I told myself there was only one solution — I needed to come up with a "million-dollar idea." Something that would give us the financial cushion we needed so I could go back to being an entrepreneur, Taylor could quit her job or work less, and we could stay in Coronado, pay off the cars, buy a home, and finally start saving money.

I spent hours every night walking around the neighborhood carrying Jovie, which was the only way she would fall asleep and stay asleep. As I did, I listened to podcasts about start-ups and entrepreneurship. Maybe I would start my own media production company. Maybe I could start a "Fulfillment by Amazon," or FBA, business; those seemed all the rage. I read about cryptocurrency and real estate flipping. For months, I kept searching for my million-dollar idea. I just needed one big lucky break so that we could cash out and start living the stress-free lives we were meant to live.

■■■■

On Monday, February 13, 2017, I woke up, kissed Taylor and Jovie goodbye, and headed out the door for work. As the line of cars stretched ahead of me on the freeway, I turned on my favorite podcast, *The Tim Ferriss Show*. Ferriss always has interesting guests and is known as a lifestyle and "life hack" guru. He's also a successful angel investor and famous for writing *The 4-Hour Workweek* and, more recently, *Tools of Titans*. His podcast description says, "I deconstruct world-class performers from eclectic areas (investing, sports, business, art, etc.) to extract tactics, tools and routines you can use." Past guests have included Arnold Schwarzenegger, Seth Godin, Amanda Palmer, Jamie Foxx, and Tony Robbins.

I was curious about this episode's odd title, "Mr. Money Mustache — Living Beautifully on $25–27K Per Year." I pressed Play. Mr. Money Mustache, whose real name is Pete Adeney, is a Canadian-born engineer of average means who retired at thirty; lives near Boulder, Colorado, with his family; and hasn't held a "real" job since 2005. In the podcast introduction, Tim asked, "How did [his family] do that? They accomplished this early retirement by doing several things, but, in effect, optimizing all aspects of their lifestyle for maximal fun, at minimal expense, and by using index fund and real estate investing. Their annual expenses total a mere $25,000 to $27,000, and they do not feel in want of anything." I did a quick mental calculation: Taylor and I were burning through this guy's annual spending in about three months! Whoa. Tim termed the Mr. Money Mustache community and philosophy "a worldwide cult phenomenon" — the blog has 300 million page views since its inception in 2011 — and he addressed Pete by telling him that he was "in the top-five most-requested guests for this podcast." That had my attention.

Pete explained that all he'd done was live like he was in college even after he was making a good salary as an engineer. Over the years, he had saved a total of between twenty-five and twenty-eight times his annual spending and invested that money in Vanguard index funds (which wouldn't be the last time I'd hear that recommendation!). Then, at thirty years old, Pete and his wife quit their cubicle jobs when their baby boy was born, since their investments were now creating enough passive income to recover their living expenses. He went on to say that this same basic formula works for most people. So all Taylor and I needed to do to retire was save twenty-five times our annual expenses? At the time, we were spending around $10,000 a month, which totaled about $120,000 a year, so that meant we needed to save a total of $3 million. That was all? Hadn't someone once calculated you needed to save, like, $10 million to retire?! That's what I had heard once from a friend, or was it on TV? I didn't remember. While I had no idea how this math worked, Pete explained it with such confidence that I was immediately intrigued.

Pete talked about how he bikes and walks for 90 percent of his trips and lives completely debt-free. He only makes purchases that remove a significant negative from his life. He drives an older car that he owns outright and uses for hauling lumber from Home Depot. Instead of pinching pennies and only buying discounted food, he buys craft beer and organic chocolate. He said, "I set my spending limit for maximum happiness, and then stop spending when those purchases stop making me happy."

I was so engrossed in the podcast that I got off the freeway, pulled under a shady tree, and texted my coworkers that I was running late because of "childcare issues." I turned up the volume and kept listening. Pete said that he chronicled his family's lifestyle on his *Mr. Money Mustache* blog, and he'd amassed a following of converts who called themselves "Mustachians." Since Pete was my first introduction to FIRE, I assumed that he'd invented the concept. Later I discovered that Pete was actually one of dozens of high-profile figures in the FIRE community and that the tenets of FIRE had existed for decades.

At one point, Ferriss remarked that this kind of lifestyle seemed like the obvious way to deal with our overwhelmingly consumerist culture. I thought about our three-bedroom house stuffed with furniture, electronics, and baby gear. Taylor and I joked that we were "Amazon addicts" because every few days a new brown package would appear on our doorstep. Who were we? Why were we living this way? Where was the couple who just wanted to have fun and enjoy the outdoors?

Pete's life sounded like the ideal grown-up life to me. I wanted to spend Monday mornings hiking in the mountains and take camping trips with my kids, to brew beer in the garage with friends and devote whole days to creative pursuits. I wanted a life without a work phone, without fluorescent lighting, without quarterly review meetings or paid time off.

Was FIRE the answer, the way for Taylor and me to spend more time with Jovie and return to doing the things we'd loved before making and spending money had become our entire focus? Would this get us back to the couple we used to be: chasing adventure, relaxed, joyful, and hopeful for the future?

Something shifted inside me. Maybe I didn't need to stumble on the "next big thing" to solve our financial concerns. Maybe our path to freedom was as simple as spending less and living more simply. For the first time in months, I felt excited. Hopeful. Energized. I had found my million-dollar idea.

THE 4 PERCENT RULE

According to the FIRE formula, once you have saved twenty-five times your annual expenses, you are ready to retire. How is that possible?

Let's say you spend $50,000 a year. That means you need to save and invest $1.25 million to retire. You can safely expect a 5 percent return on your investments, which for $1.25 million would be $62,500 a year (this is a very conservative assumption, and in most years, your returns will be higher). This is actually more than the $50,000 you need! However, each year, if you only withdraw 4 percent of the income your investments earn (or $50,000), this means you always have a buffer to make up for inflation and dips in the market. The "4 percent rule," also referred to as the "safe withdrawal rate," is based on a Trinity University study, and it is used to determine the dollar amount a retiree can pull from savings each year without decreasing, or drawing down, on the principal.

Here's the math one more time: If you save twenty-five times your annual spending, and then invest it so you get a 5 percent return on average after inflation, you can live off those investments for eternity if you only withdraw 4 percent a year.

If you still have questions, don't worry. I will explain the math in more detail as we go.

CHAPTER 2

THE MILLION-DOLLAR IDEA

Up until that Monday in February, I had found my work life less and less tolerable. Traveling constantly, hustling to video shoots, hauling heavy gear, and regularly pulling twelve-hour days to finish a shoot were a young man's game, and I was starting to feel my age more and more. That said, my coworkers were like family, I was consistently challenged, and I was good at my job. Still, I didn't always love the ever-increasing responsibilities: the pressure to perform at increasingly high levels; the hours spent growing our customer base, crunching numbers, and sitting at a desk. Whether I was growing a video production company or working at a creative agency, the higher up the ladder I went, the more stress I seemed to encounter.

Now that I knew a forty-year-old dude in Colorado was spending his Mondays going hiking and reading a book on his porch, it felt unbearable to have to put up with all the things I didn't like about my work. A weeklong conference now meant a week away from my baby and more sleepless nights. Every hour spent inside creating proposals and looking out my window at the California sunshine was torture.

My favorite time of day was in the evenings, when I would walk with Jovie to help her fall asleep. Once Jovie and Taylor were snoozing, I would spend hours researching and reading about Mr. Money Mustache and all the other amazing people who were talking about FIRE. In fact, as I googled articles about *early retirement* and *financial independence*, I realized there were thousands of other people doing this.

I read about a couple who retired in their thirties with three kids. A man who put aside 70 percent of his IT salary to retire at thirty-five so he could drive around the country in an RV. A couple who got rid of their house and four cars and started living in a manufactured home. I read about a couple who used real estate investing to quit their jobs at age twenty-nine so they could travel the world before having a baby. Then they had a baby and *kept* traveling — and now their five-month-old had been to more countries than I had! I tried to imagine us living that kind of a life: Jovie in front of the pyramids, swimming in the Caribbean, visiting the Great Wall of China. This was a far cry from the nine-to-five grind, living for the weekend.

Pete from *Mr. Money Mustache* was just one "guide" for the FIRE movement. Dozens of bloggers were chronicling their journeys to financial independence. Some remained anonymous to protect their corporate careers; some were already "retired"; some were financially independent but had decided to keep working; and some were planning to quit their jobs as soon as possible, in weeks or even days. Many of these blogs are still going strong (these are listed in the boxed text on page 26, and more resources are available at playingwithfire.co). Jacob Lund Fiske from *Early Retirement Extreme* is a physicist who became financially independent through extreme frugality and managed to live off of $7,000 a year in the San Francisco Bay Area by living in his RV and wearing the same clothes for ten-plus years. Liz and Nate Thames from *Frugalwoods* left their expensive lifestyle in Cambridge and bought a homestead in Vermont, where they are living frugally by growing their own food and doing yearlong "spending bans." Julien and Kiersten Saunders from *Rich & Regular* are a couple from Atlanta who went from amassing consumer debt to paying off their mortgage. Brandon Ganch from *Mad Fientist* is a former software engineer who retired at thirty-four and lives in Scotland. Jeremy Jacobsen and Winnie Tseng from *Go*

Curry Cracker! specialize in international "geo-arbitrage" — living in exotic low-cost locales around the world. Today, there is a blogger offering advice for every kind of FIRE lifestyle: for people with kids, for military families, for living in big cities, for traveling around the world, for donating time to charitable causes, and so on. At the time, I was amazed that so many people knew about this idea, and I'd never even heard of it.

POPULAR FIRE BLOGS

Mr. Money Mustache: mrmoneymustache.com

Mad Fientist: madfientist.com

Frugalwoods: frugalwoods.com

Physician on Fire: physicianonfire.com

Early Retirement Extreme: earlyretirementextreme.com

The Simple Path to Wealth: jlcollinsnh.com

Millennial Revolution: millennial-revolution.com

ChooseFI: choosefi.com

Afford Anything: affordanything.com

Inclusion on this list is based on 2018 Alexa rankings.

A couple of years before, I'd been excited about starting my own podcast project, which I'd dropped because I couldn't find the time. If we could achieve FIRE, maybe I'd become a podcaster. Maybe I'd finally be able to donate my time to causes I believed in, like the Ocean Cleanup project or raising awareness of the Effective Altruism movement. Maybe Taylor would have the time to pursue some of her passions — like volunteering at a senior center or starting a nonprofit helping single moms. I thought about getting to eat lunch with my wife and daughter more often. Waking up without a schedule. Spending winters in the Caribbean and summers in Lake Tahoe. All the moments I wanted to have with Jovie before she was grown — teaching her how to surf, showing her the reefs off the coast of Belize, hiking the Pacific Crest Trail, coaching her soccer team, and learning to play piano together.

When Taylor asked me why I was so distracted, I would mumble something about a challenging project at work and then scurry off, laptop in hand. The truth was that even though I knew I would tell her eventually, I didn't want to overwhelm her or have her think that this was just another one of my far-fetched "big ideas." I knew that this idea was different. Unlike my other (weekly) ideas, this one didn't involve starting yet another business or risking time and money. This was about taking the money we were already making and using it more effectively. And I was quickly becoming convinced that FIRE *was* my million-dollar idea and our best chance to live the life we wanted: more time outdoors, more time together, more time with Jovie.

In our relationship, I was always the frugal one. Some of our most memorable fights had been about or related to money. This was especially true early in our relationship, when it had first become apparent how differently Taylor and I thought about money. After growing up as a navy brat for most of my early years, I was raised in a Midwest community where frugality was part of the local identity; saving money was praised as smart and made you "like the rest of us." When I got a good deal on a hotel room or bought a computer on clearance, I was eager and proud to tell people about it! This really embarrassed Taylor. Taylor had been raised to feel like talking about saving money or bragging about a "good deal" was tacky, a sign that you couldn't afford to pay full price. On the other hand, she had no problem talking about expensive purchases or showing off luxuries, which in turn drove me crazy. In my family, flaunting wealth is considered pretentious, a sign that you think you are better than other people. For Taylor, these purchases were a sign of her hard work and nothing to feel ashamed of.

Eventually, Taylor and I both adapted by not discussing it anymore: I stopped sharing how little I was paying for things, and she stopped sharing how much she spent on something. That's why I assumed that if I brought up FIRE too casually, Taylor might see it as a judgment of her financial attitudes or a way to deprive us of luxuries we enjoyed. Besides, who was I to tell her how she should spend money when she made more than I did?

On the other hand, Taylor wanted to stay home with Jovie, and doing that meant changing our approach to finances. I felt that once she understood that FIRE was about cutting back to have more — especially more time with family — she would be on board. So I did what any sane person does when they're afraid to have a tough conversation with their spouse: I sent her an email. In the subject line, I wrote "Check out this article," and in the body of the email, I pasted a link to a blog post written by Mr. Money Mustache that described the math behind FIRE. This was one of my favorites from the hundreds of posts I had read. I was pretty sure this particular article would really stand out to her.

That night while we cooked dinner, I kept waiting for her to bring it up. Did she think it was weird? Was she as excited as I was? I couldn't wait to share everything I had learned with her and show her all the ways I thought we could cut back on our lifestyle costs. But she didn't mention the email. Not while we cooked, not while we ate, not even after dinner while we did the dishes. Finally, when we were about to go to sleep, I brought it up.

"Oh yeah," she said. "I didn't read the whole thing, but it seemed interesting." Then she mentioned something about

Jovie's playdate with a new friend. Clearly, my wife had not caught the FIRE bug. I had more work to do.

■ ■ ■ ■

Taylor wasn't the only person with whom I shared my new obsession with FIRE. A week after I first heard Mr. Money Mustache's interview, I bounced the idea off of a close friend, Joe. He was a former coworker and somebody I looked up to. He seemed financially responsible, and he had helped me vet a number of business ideas in the past. I felt I could safely test the waters with him in preparation for pitching FIRE to my wife, since he was good at gently talking me off the ledge.

As soon as he answered his phone, I launched into it: I had discovered the secret to happiness, which was to spend way less than you made and save all the extra and then live off the dividends and travel the world and spend every day frolicking in a field, which I learned about through this guy named Mr. Money Mustache — yes, that's a real name — and oh my god, dude, you have to read this guy's blog; it will blow your mind.

"Oh yeah, I've heard of that guy," Joe said.

I was speechless. He'd already heard of the secret to happiness?!

Turned out Joe had been reading Mr. Money Mustache's blog for years.

"Why didn't you tell me?" I demanded. "You knew about this all along, and you didn't say anything?"

"Well, you and I don't talk about that kind of stuff," Joe said. He was right. We talked about many personal topics — business ideas, politics, health — but (like most people) we'd never really discussed money or lifestyle choices.

It occurred to me that in the four years I had known Joe, he had often ridden his bike to work. He owned a used Honda Fit. He and his wife, Angel, lived in a neighborhood that was nice but much more affordable than mine. And whenever we spent time together, he usually suggested we do something at one of our houses instead of going out. This whole time, one of my closest friends was living a FIRE lifestyle, and I hadn't even noticed.

My conversation with Joe convinced me even further that Taylor and I needed to get serious about this. We both looked up to Joe and Angel because of the calm, relaxed way they lived their lives. They enjoyed the simple things in life that we were often too busy for, and they were two of the happiest, most content people we knew.

The problem was that I still didn't know how to approach this topic with Taylor without it turning into a fight about money. In the past, I'd often taken the wrong tone when discussing our spending. I'd obsess about a random purchase ("Why did we spend $1,400 on paddleboards?!") or get upset about an expensive gift we'd bought for a baby shower. Taylor would rightfully point out that I was just as much to blame: I'd originally wanted the paddleboards, and I'd agreed to the gift. Then we'd fight about who was the bigger spender and who was more at fault for not sticking with a budget. Sometimes we would stick to a budget for a few months, but then a vacation would come up, we'd get too busy to cook, we'd have to fly to a wedding, and slowly but surely, frugality went out the window.

This time, I didn't want to nag. I didn't want Taylor to become defensive and disgruntled. I wanted Taylor to see FIRE the way I saw it: as a way to work less, have less stress, and finally get on the path we had always wanted for ourselves — doing what we wanted, when we wanted! Who wouldn't want that? Pure and utter freedom! Freedom of choice, freedom from financial stress, freedom to just be! I decided my best strategy was to keep sending her links to articles and podcast interviews and see if anything stuck.

Over the next week, that's what I did. I sent her *Mad Fientist* and *ChooseFI* podcasts, articles by the Frugalwoods, and posts from Mr. Money Mustache. She'd mention one occasionally, but mostly she was too busy to read or listen to them. The material wasn't catching on with her, and I was getting frustrated. At this rate, we were going to be retirement age before I convinced Taylor to retire early.

CHAPTER 3

TEN THINGS THAT MAKE YOU HAPPY

As I struggled with how to truly broach the topic of FIRE with Taylor, I didn't realize how many couples wrestle with the same dilemma. Since then, I've heard dozens of stories about how one spouse has tried (and in some cases, failed) to convince the other spouse about the amazing possibilities of FIRE. For instance, there is Brandon from the *Mad Fientist* blog. In the early years of his relationship with his wife, Jill, Brandon was so extreme about FIRE and frugality that Jill decided she wanted nothing to do with it. Today, years later, they are both FIRE advocates, but clearly, convincing your spouse can be a real obstacle on the road to financial independence, and it needs to be done thoughtfully and respectfully.

The truth of our situation was that I couldn't pursue FIRE without Taylor. Not only was she earning more than half of our income, but she was the mother of my child and my life partner. If she didn't agree to cutting costs and making big life-style changes, it would be a lonely road for me.

One day, it occurred to me that if I wanted Taylor to get excited about what FIRE would give us (less work, less financial stress, more fun, more time with Jovie) and not focus on what FIRE meant doing without (like new cars, restaurant dinners, and so on), then I needed to start by getting us both focused on the positive things we already valued the most.

One night, as we were washing the dishes after dinner, I asked Taylor to do me a favor and write down the top ten things that made her happy on a weekly basis. When she asked why, I told her it was an exercise related to all this FIRE stuff I had been sending her way, plus I thought it would be fun to compare our lists. She agreed, and I went to give Jovie a bath and put her to sleep. Immediately, I started to doubt my plan. What if Taylor wrote, *Driving my BMW* or *Going out to expensive dinners?* What if she doubled down on the island lifestyle or the beach? What if I had just done the worst thing possible, which was remind my wife of everything she loved right before suggesting that we give it all up?

As soon as I walked into our bedroom, Taylor asked if I wanted to hear her list. Here's what she wrote:

1. Hearing my baby laugh
2. Having coffee with my husband
3. Cuddling with my baby
4. Going for a walk
5. Going for a bike ride
6. Enjoying a glass of wine
7. Good chocolate
8. Talking to my parents and family
9. Having family dinners
10. Reading to my baby

Hearing that list reminded me of why Taylor and I fell in love in the first place; she and I both value family and experiences above all else. We had gotten offtrack somehow and become convinced that we had to spend money to enjoy life. But it was clear after hearing her list that we both still valued the same things. I was so relieved. Everything on that list was possible living a frugal lifestyle.

It was also uncanny how similar our lists were. Here was mine:

1. Reading to Jovie until she falls asleep
2. Listening to music
3. Enjoying libations
4. Having coffee with Tay

5. Spending time outdoors (riding bikes, going hiking, etc.)
6. Cooking dinner for the family
7. Reading
8. Spending time with friends
9. Playing competitive sports
10. Fishing

I told her how writing my list made me realize that the things I love doing are simple and inexpensive. "What did you think when you saw your list?" I asked her.

"That the beach isn't on there." I knew by the way she said it that she and I were having the same thought: *Then why do we live in such an expensive beach town?*

"The only things that cost money on my list are wine and chocolate." I agreed.

She started naming things she had purchased in the past few months that, at the time, she felt like she deserved because of how hard she was working, but in hindsight hadn't really made her happy and certainly hadn't made her list. It was now very apparent that all the articles and podcasts I had sent along had started to seep into her subconscious.

The Ten Things Exercise ended up being one of the most meaningful elements of our decision to pursue FIRE. We both still have our lists today and reference them frequently. In fact, I recommend this approach very highly, and I have included instructions in this chapter (see "The Ten Things Exercise," page 37). The lists worked because they forced us to face an uncomfortable reality: Our spending wasn't reflecting our values. After sharing our lists, we were talking more openly about money than we ever had, and I decided to raise the idea of FIRE, or at least the idea of drastically cutting our expenses.

"You know all those articles about financial independence that I've been sending you? I've been doing a ton of reading, and I think this could make sense for us," I told her. I explained about the first podcast interview I'd heard with Mr. Money Mustache, the conversation I'd had with Joe, and all the research I'd done since. I confessed that I was totally obsessed with FIRE, much more than I'd let on, and I had a feeling that we had to pursue this.

Immediately, Taylor asked why I hadn't told her sooner. Normally, Taylor and I talk frequently about what is on our minds, and it was out of the norm that I would keep something like this from her. I explained that I had been anxious she wouldn't take it well, since spending wasn't an easy topic between us, and she already had too much on her plate with Jovie and work. Plus, FIRE would require a drastically different lifestyle — one that I wasn't sure we could manage.

Taylor listened to me without saying anything. I could tell she was trying to figure out whether this was another one of my crazy ideas or something more serious.

"You really think we can retire early?" she asked.

I nodded.

"Then I'm open to learning more."

THE TEN THINGS EXERCISE

We all have a limited amount of time on earth, and so much of that time gets taken up either trying to earn money or spending the money we earn. But what do you actually want to be doing with your time? What do you enjoy doing? What is the best possible use of your time?

The Ten Things Exercise is simple but powerful. Make a list

of the ten things you most enjoy doing on a weekly basis. You can also use a month as the time frame, but I like using a week. A typical day is too busy and full of tasks, and a month allows too much time for excessive plans and spendy ideas. What you spend your weeks doing is really what you'll spend your life doing, and that's what makes the exercise so insightful. If you are doing this exercise with a partner, try not to compare your lists until you're finished. Once you're finished, reflect on what you've written. What do you notice about these ten activities? Is there a pattern or theme? What's not included?

Extra credit: Make a list of the ten things you spend the most money on every month, and compare it with the list of your ten favorite activities. Are you spending your money on the things you actually enjoy?

Over the next few days, Taylor and I discussed FIRE at length. She was interested and open to the ideas, but she didn't like how extreme it all sounded: How were we going to go from our current lifestyle to eating rice and beans and living in a camper? If it was so "easy" to save half of what you earn and retire within around ten years, why wasn't everyone doing this?! Was it even possible for us to save half of what we earned?

I didn't have answers to all her questions, but I was sure if we got started, we'd find a way. After all, we both agreed that our current lifestyle wasn't working.

What really changed Taylor's thinking was an episode of the *ChooseFI* podcast called "The Pillars of FI." This discussion singlehandedly converted FIRE from a curiosity into a serious possibility that truly excited Taylor about what FIRE could mean for us. She felt like she finally understood the "why" behind frugality, the philosophy of the movement. She played me what, for her, was the key statement of the episode: when one of the hosts, Brad Barrett, says, "We're not making any proclamation on how you should be living your life. Think a little bit differently." Taylor responded to the idea that FIRE is not inherently about being extreme. It's simply about trying to pursue financial independence. The speed at which you get there and the choices you make along the way are up to you. Once she felt more encouraged that she could pursue FIRE in her own way, we decided to dig into our numbers.

We sat at the kitchen table, and I showed her two calculations that I had done the week before using a tool called a retirement calculator I had found online. I based the calculations on our 2016 tax return. That year, our after-tax income was $142,000, our total expenditures were $132,000 (which included $10,000 we'd spent to finally pay off my student loans), and we saved a little over $10,000. One of the calculations showed when we could retire if we kept going the way we were going. I chose to set our spending at about $120,000 a year (or $10,000 a month). The other calculator showed when we could retire if we cut our expenses in half and spent only $60,000 a year. I had followed the FIRE math exactly, so both of the calculations assumed a 5 percent return on investment and a 4 percent withdrawal rate.

HOW DOES A
RETIREMENT CALCULATOR WORK?

A retirement calculator works by taking your current income and subtracting your current annual expenses to figure out your savings rate. Based on that savings rate, the calculator figures out how many years you'll need to work to save enough money so that the annual income from your investments will cover your living expenses.

There are some great calculators online specifically geared for early retirement, but I also decided to create a *Playing with*

FIRE calculator for readers who are curious to plug in their own numbers and see their retirement dates in an easy-to-use interface. The PWF calculator is simple, not perfect. It doesn't currently factor in how your income and expenses will change over time, such as once your house is paid off, and so on. But I think it's a great jumping-off point and we plan to update it in the future. You can check it out here: playingwithfire.co/retirementcalculator

YOU CAN RETIRE IN	**34.3 YEARS**
WITH A SAVINGS RATE OF	**16%**
ANNUAL EXPENSES	120,000
ANNUAL SAVINGS	22,000
MONTHLY EXPENSES	10,000
MONTHLY SAVINGS	1,833

YOU CAN RETIRE IN	**11 YEARS**
WITH A SAVINGS RATE OF	**58%**
ANNUAL EXPENSES	60,000
ANNUAL SAVINGS	82,000
MONTHLY EXPENSES	5,000
MONTHLY SAVINGS	6,833

I explained the calculations. In this case, if we spent $60,000 a year, we'd need to save $1.5 million for the income from our investments to pay for our lifestyle. How long would it take to save that much money? According to my calculation, it would be eleven years if we saved $82,000 annually. If our incomes increased or we could lower our expenses below $60,000, we could get there even faster. Conversely, if our income dropped, we would save less, and it could take longer.

"What about inflation? What if the stock market crashes?" Taylor asked. We both had seen friends lose jobs and houses during the 2008 recession, and we didn't want to risk that happening to us.

I explained that all this math is based on a 5 percent rate of return on investments — most years, the stock market returns are much higher than that and some years less. And it also assumes a 4 percent withdrawal rate. Ideally, the 1 percent difference provides a buffer to protect you against inflation and normal fluctuations in the market. However, this is separate from a genuine market crash (see the box below).

"There are hundreds of people out there who have done this," I told her. "Some of them have been retired for decades."

WHAT ACTUALLY HAPPENS IF THE STOCK MARKET CRASHES?

You may be thinking what Taylor was thinking: What happens if the stock market crashes and your investments lose most or all of their value? Then you may be out of money, out of a job, and basically out of luck.

The math behind FIRE isn't foolproof and cannot predict what will happen if we are faced with a global financial catastrophe. But the equation does work perfectly...most of the time under normal circumstances. In fact, according to the Trinity University study cited earlier, a 4 percent withdrawal rate works 98 percent of the time over a thirty-year projection.

The first time I read that, I thought, *Well, what happens if my family is one of the 2 percent that it doesn't work for? And if we retire in our forties, our retirement window will hopefully be much longer than thirty years.* One common answer for that is, if you're concerned about the risk, save thirty-five times your annual expenses, and use a 3.25 percent "safe withdrawal rate." That means you have to save more before you retire, but it gives you a bigger cushion in times of financial crisis.

In addition, FIRE doesn't force you to retire once you reach your savings goals. Taylor and I both plan on working (in some form or another) once we reach financial independence, and even a small income should be enough to support us if the stock market dips.

Social Security is yet another cushion. Most people pursuing FIRE leave it out of their projections, so it becomes an added financial buffer if or when it kicks in. Additionally, if you fall short of your savings goals, or if the wider financial landscape does not cooperate, continuing to work or to lower expenses will hopefully get you through any rough patches. All of this alleviates the need to get it perfect.

"So you're saying that I could quit my job in eleven years?"

I nodded. If we cut our expenses by 50 percent, we would be retired in our forties.

She looked up at me. "I'm in," she said. "Let's do this."

I felt a giant weight lift off my shoulders. This was how I wanted it to be: taking on big adventures, side by side, ready to face whatever happens together.

"But I'm not giving up the BMW."

All right, we still had work to do. But it was a good start.

TAYLOR'S TAKE: COMING TO TERMS WITH FIRE

In this book, I asked Taylor to share her perspective on our experiences with FIRE, and throughout I've included boxes in which she tells her side of the story. Here is what she said about making the decision to pursue FIRE:

■ ■ ■ ■

When it came to finances, I used to be blissfully ignorant. I've always believed in fun and spontaneity being the key to a happy life, and that occasionally has led to a big bar tab or plane ticket or car payment or Nordstrom bill...you get the point! I love life. I love paying the bill for my friends when we go out. I love trying new restaurants. I love last-minute weekend trips. My belief has always been that if we're not going into debt, we're doing fine.

So when I first started reading about FIRE, I felt pretty unenthused. Not only did I love driving my beautiful car and enjoying nice things, but I didn't like all the mocking of how "stupid consumers" were "wasting their money." I felt like whoever these "FI" people were, they weren't going to like me.

Then Scott sent me a podcast called *ChooseFI*. During the first episode I listened to, the hosts, Brad Barrett and Jonathan Mendonsa, described how every person's path to financial independence is different. It doesn't make my way better or your way worse; it's just whatever works for you. They said they were trying to give listeners some guidelines to jump off with, not tell them what to do. I loved that approach — it was so much more appealing and approachable than some of the other material I was reading. It didn't make me feel bad for having all my things or living in the place I lived.

The thing that finally changed my mind was seeing the

numbers written out. If we kept going the way we were going, I was going to be working for the rest of my life. I was going to miss out on the chance to spend time with Scott and Jovie. That wasn't what I wanted.

How Our Family of Seven Reached FI with an Average Income of $60,000

While filming the *Playing with FIRE* documentary, I had the chance to meet hundreds of people who were on this FIRE journey with us, and I've included some of these interviews in this book.

By the Numbers

Pre-FI career: Sales
Current Age: 35
Age at FI: 32
Current annual spending: $30,000

What FIRE Means to Me

Growing up under the poverty line, I quickly understood how money gives you options and freedom. I had a number of adverse childhood experiences growing up. At one point, I begged my mom to leave an unhealthy marriage, but she was worried about supporting us kids on her own. I felt stuck. As soon as I could afford it, I moved out and started supporting myself.

My Path to FIRE

My husband, Adam, and I got married a year after high school. I had saved $8,000 during high school, which I used to buy a camper that I lived in, and Adam and I lived in it for the first year of our marriage. He had $45,000 in debt, and this was shortly followed by another $10,000 of medical expenses from being a teenager without insurance. So our FIRE journey started with $55,000 of debt, a twenty-year-old camper, and a pieced-together Geo Metro. Not the most glamorous jumping-off point. Adam joined the army to pay off his student loan debt, and then we lived as frugally as possible using just his income and saving mine. We had a roommate and only took camping vacations. By twenty-one, we had paid off all the debt, and by twenty-four, we had saved our first $100,000.

After ten years, Adam retired as a sergeant with a $1,450 monthly military pension. After he retired from the army, we both kept working, and we saved enough money to buy a house with cash and then two rental properties. We always wanted to be financially independent, but we also had big dreams. We wanted to take mini-retirements, long-term sabbaticals to taste what life was like after FI. We wanted to travel the world, and we wanted to adopt. We knew our path to FI had to include all those things, so along the way, we took four mini-retirements, ranging from one month up to a year, traveled to twenty-seven countries, lived abroad, adopted four kids, and had two biological kids.

In a Nutshell

✓ It took us thirteen years to reach FI with an average annual income of $60,000.

✓ We took four mini-retirements along the way to travel, adopt our children, and build passive income with rentals.

✓ We live off Adam's army pension, our rental income, and our investments.

✓ Early retirement has given us the resources and ability to adopt four foster kids.

✓ We paid cash for a $50,000 fixer house and did most of the renovating ourselves.

The Hardest Part

Retiring in our thirties has put a strain on some of our friendships. A lot of people get really confused about it, especially since we were never particularly high earners. It's hard to lose these old relationships as we grow and change. Some people are very supportive and understand how we are using FI to live our best life. Other relationships have become distant because we are in a different phase of life than the other parties are.

The Best Part

Without a doubt, the most valuable thing our FIRE journey has given us is the ability to adopt three siblings. No foster family before us had been able to keep all three of the kids together. Because we have had the freedom to travel and prioritize family, the kids are flourishing. It feels like they have always been with us.

My Advice to You

Start now by gaining a clear vision for what you want out of this life. So much of our wealth has come from the power of saving, investing early, and taking calculated risks with rentals.

FIRE STORY: JILLIAN ▪ KALISPELL, MT

CHAPTER 4

I SPEND HOW MUCH ON COFFEE?!

Once we decided to adopt the FIRE mindset, we knew we needed a plan to cut back on spending. To make this plan, we relied heavily on a post written by Mr. Money Mustache titled "The Shockingly Simple Math Behind Early Retirement," which says that the only math that matters is comparing how much you're earning versus how much you're spending. If you're saving 60 percent of what you take home in your paycheck, you can retire in about ten years. So how were we going to save 60 percent when we were currently saving less than 10 percent (and occasionally dipping into those savings for travel and big purchases)? Most people pursuing FIRE focused on a few key expenses, often called "The Big Three": housing, transportation, and food. Two of those seemed off-limits: We had a two-year lease on our rental house, so we weren't moving, and we weren't getting rid of our new cars. I had scored a damn good deal on my leased Mazda, and Taylor made it clear she was not willing to negotiate the BMW lease.

Here is the ten-step plan we came up with:

1. Cut down on "fun" spending, like Amazon purchases, electronics, clothes, toys for Jovie, and so on.
2. Stop eating out. Eat breakfast and dinner at home, and pack lunches for work.
3. Review monthly expenses like internet, Netflix, Hulu, HBO, phone bill, gym memberships, Jovie's swim lessons, and so on.
4. Keep entertainment free or low cost, like walks

on the beach, movies at home, and potlucks with friends.

5. Sell anything in the house that we don't use or need.

6. Search for a less-expensive childcare option, like daycare or a shared nanny.

7. Start biking whenever possible, including for Scott's commute to work.

8. Take fewer vacations and utilize credit card rewards to pay for them.

9. When the lease on our house is up, find a cheaper place to live.

10. Look for extra-income possibilities, like Scott picking up occasional freelance gigs and Taylor trying to max out her commission opportunities.

In addition, we had to figure out how much money we were spending and what we were spending it on. I knew this was going to be eye-opening.

Up until now, we had managed to keep our heads above water, but that wasn't thanks to strategic planning. Simply put, we were winging it. To make matters more blurry, Taylor worked on commission, and for most of my career, I had worked on a project basis, so our earnings were inconsistent. Instead of saving more aggressively to provide a buffer for the leaner months, we always just spent like it was going to be a good month. We optimistically convinced ourselves that we'd make more when we needed it, and in retrospect, we were extremely lucky to have increased earnings without any major catastrophic financial losses.

Before we could figure out a livable FIRE-friendly budget, we had to catalog our current expenses. This wasn't the first time I had attempted to review our expenses, but I always viewed the practice as a nightmare chore that I'd rather put off for another day (or another year) — partly because I was afraid of what I'd find and partly because I'd convinced myself that since we worked so hard and made such good incomes, we didn't need to bother ourselves with the small stuff. Now we had to come face-to-face with the small stuff. But this time felt different. With FIRE as the end goal, Taylor and I blocked off three hours on a Saturday morning in early March, braced ourselves for the worst, and dove in.

RIECKENS FAMILY AVERAGE MONTHLY EXPENSES

Here is the breakdown of our average monthly expenses, which we divided into a few broad categories. Some expenses, like housing and groceries, were averages over the year, and others were specific to February 2017 (the most recent full month). We deliberately left out health insurance and state and federal taxes, since these were already withheld from our paychecks (and didn't represent "spending" out of our take-home pay). Below, totals are rounded to simplify the math.

Rent	$3,000
Childcare	$2,500
Car leases	$650
Car insurance and gas	$600
Utilities	$150
Medical co-pays and prescriptions	$140
Cell phone and internet	$300
Groceries	$1,000
Eating out	$1,100
Boat club	$350
Entertainment	$450
Miscellaneous	$100

In total, our average monthly expenses were $10,340, which came to $124,080 for the year. We may have been making good money, but we were still technically living paycheck to paycheck. I'd been ignoring this fact for a long time, but there it was in black and white. This wasn't sustainable. If one of us was laid off or we had a big unexpected expense, we'd be in serious trouble.

More than just lowering our total expenses, our goal with FIRE was to bring our values in line with how we were spending our money. As we looked at the evidence, one thing became starkly apparent: We were not being the best custodians of our future. Philosophically, both Taylor and I valued simplicity and minimalism, but in practice, we were overspending and undersaving in ways that valued momentary satisfaction over long-term stability.

By dividing our monthly expenses by thirty, we figured we were spending, on average, $345 a day. We had a problem that we had been nonchalantly sweeping under the $750 rug we had bought on sale at West Elm (which was originally $1,000 — a steal!). We were spending way too much on things we did not need and then feeling deprived of the things we wanted most, like adventure, relaxation, and time together. The cumulation of our life energy was all around us: the furniture, the fancy blender, a flat-screen TV, a $50 bottle of wine. The cost of those things was more than just a number; it was our peace of mind.

Further, our report showed, much to my chagrin, that we were both equally at fault. I might have told myself I was the frugal one, but the evidence wasn't there. While Taylor enjoyed clothes shopping at Nordstrom and made BMW lease payments, I enjoyed expensive lunches and technology and made boat club membership payments. I considered our entertainment spending: $450 a month. What kind of entertainment were we possibly spending $450 on? It dawned on me that I was living in San Diego, where an amazing amount of free outdoor entertainment is readily available.

We were spending $2,100 a month on food or about $70 a day. I had recently read an article about how one couple pursuing FIRE cooked at home for less than $10 a day. How were we going to get from $70 to $10? Staring at these embarrassing and lavish expenses, I found myself getting defensive. I thought: *It's perfectly reasonable to spend $549 on a blender. And we need two cars! We live in San Diego!* For every expense I knew we could cut back on, there was another I felt sure we couldn't live without.

"We're still saving, though, right?" Taylor asked.

We were, but not much. As stated above, the previous year, in 2016, Taylor and I made a combined $142,000 after taxes. Our yearly expenses in 2016 were about $132,000, which meant we'd saved about $10,000 that year, which was about our average. Up to now, I'd always felt, in a vague sort of way, that we didn't need to watch the bottom line too closely because we had almost $190,000 in total savings, which included Taylor's 401k and proceeds from my business parked in a Roth IRA.

Now, I could no longer ignore the realities and missteps of our spending habits and the long-term harm it was causing our family. I suddenly saw clearly how our previous definition of a dream life (living by the beach, buying the newest technology, dining at the fanciest restaurants) wasn't actually a dream life: Our true dream life was to be free from the burden of paying for all of this.

Most importantly, our assumption that we were "relatively responsible" with our spending was totally false. To change, we would need to start tracking our daily expenses going forward. We were using our savings to pay for a lot of needless "one-time" expenses — a drone that I thought I needed for work! A brand-new digital crib for Jovie! A weekend trip to Chicago! For some reason, we had never considered these types of "unusual" expenses part of our monthly budget, but from now on, we needed to.

If I was honest with myself, I had to admit I'd been naïvely hoping that this exercise would actually reveal that we were much smarter spenders than we'd thought and that, with a couple of modest tweaks, we could easily cut our spending in half. Instead I'd come face-to-face with a rude reality: We were pretty far offtrack.

■ ■ ■ ■

As we considered where to make cuts in our expenses, part of our problem was that we had no idea what a more reasonable lifestyle looked like. Most of our San Diego friends lived the same type of lifestyle we did, and I would have bet our expenses were lower than a lot of our friends'! On the other hand, I knew families were living on half or even a fraction of what we were. But how? Where did they start? If we wanted to reach financial independence as quickly as possible, and we did, I knew we had to cut our expenses to the extreme.

So we decided to focus on food. The *Frugalwoods* family wrote that they paid to eat out only two times a year. Brad from the *ChooseFI* podcast mentioned that his wife learned to cook meals that cost two dollars per person. And Pete from *Mr. Money Mustache* continually espoused his love for intentional trips to Costco. The advice seemed pretty clear: Stop eating out, start cooking at home, and buy in bulk.

Up till then, my morning routine was to pick up a coffee and a breakfast sandwich every day at Starbucks. These were the first expenses to go. The daily coffee was especially embarrassing, since my work supplied free fair-trade coffee and cold brew on tap to all their employees. Then, for breakfast, I stocked up on eggs and tortillas at Costco and made myself a stash of frozen breakfast burritos that I could take to work.

To figure out what that change was actually "worth" to me, I used the "Latte Factor Calculator" created by Financial Mentor. This calculator quantifies the true cost of small, seemingly inconsequential expenses over long periods of time. In essence, it tells you what the same amount of money would earn over the same time period if it were invested (and earning compound interest) rather than spent. Here is what my Starbucks habit would have cost us if I hadn't changed:

Monthly cost of daily Starbucks coffee and sandwich: $160
Yearly average cost ($160 x 12 months): $1,920
Cost over thirty years: $57,600
Earnings over thirty years if same money were invested (assuming 5% return and compounding interest): $133,161

The next things we tackled were lunches and dinners. Over the years, it had become normal for Taylor and me to buy lunch nearly every day and go out to eat or order takeout many nights. We didn't even think about cooking; we just assumed we wouldn't be eating at home. Now we pledged to do the complete opposite, and I started cooking bigger dinners so that I could bring leftovers to work the next day. We created meal plans and bought as many ingredients as possible at Costco. It was amazing seeing how the small things — combining trips to the grocery store, buying in bulk, buying only what was on our list — added up to significant savings.

One of the most interesting (and totally unexpected) outcomes of bringing my own lunch to work was that my coworkers started to ask me about it. They noticed the drastic change from a daily Starbucks and purchased lunch to drinking free work coffee and eating leftovers in Tupperware. I discovered that most of my coworkers were living a much more frugal lifestyle than I had realized. I had been telling myself that it was impossible to live in Southern California on less money than we were spending, but the evidence against that was right in front of me the whole time. Most of the people I worked with brought lunches every day, and they had lots of tips and suggestions for how to cut down on food expenses. Best of all, I started telling people about FIRE and how much it was motivating me to change my lifestyle.

The trickiest part proved to be our social life. Most of our Coronado friends had jobs that were as demanding as ours, which meant that more often than not, we all met at a pub or restaurant to keep things simple. Often, we would make the outing an event and try the newest or hottest restaurant. Even if the place wasn't very fancy, Taylor and I could easily spend $70 getting food and drinks for the two of us, and when you multiply that by five or six times a month, it really added up. After our "FIRE conversion," for the first couple of dinner invitations, we either suggested inexpensive taco shops or invited other couples to our house for a home-cooked meal. But that didn't appeal to all our friends all the time.

The first time we dealt with this problem was when our friends Josh and Steph invited us to get sushi one weekend. Josh and Steph both had high-powered jobs and clearly made a lot more money than we did. They lived in a beautiful home with views of the Pacific Ocean. Before FIRE, Taylor and I would have thought nothing of dropping $80 each on a sushi dinner, but now indulging in that kind of meal felt like we'd be giving up on our FIRE decision. I tried to convince Josh to do something a little more frugal. I texted him and suggested a more casual restaurant near their house, but he said they'd just been there last week. Then I invited them to come over to our house instead, but he said they were really craving sushi.

Later, Taylor suggested, "Maybe we should just go and order less?" We decided to go but skip the wine, and we'd eat a snack before leaving the house so we weren't starving.

I felt awkward when Steph suggested getting a bottle of wine and Taylor and I declined; we said we weren't drinking. After a lifetime of saying yes to any and all merriment, it seemed out of character to be so disciplined. I hated the feeling that we were coming off as cheap or that we were casting a pall on the evening by not joining in the fun. I was proud of our newfound commitment to frugality, but I didn't have the courage to tell them what we were doing.

On the drive home, I asked Taylor if she had felt as uncomfortable as I had. She said the meal was fine — after the first fifteen minutes, she didn't even care what we were eating because the point was spending time with our friends. But she kept wondering how it looked that we were making these weird little decisions that were pretty obviously just tactics to spend less. In the future, either we had to get better at hiding, we had to avoid these kinds of outings, or we had to come clean with all our friends so they weren't confused. We decided that hiding was a terrible idea, and avoiding outings would only ensure we saw our friends much less. Coming clean made the most sense, and perhaps that would naturally lead to our friends suggesting cheaper options on our behalf, like game nights and eating in. Maybe we were being naïve, but we hoped that our friends might want to join us and hop on the FIRE train too.

Overall, cutting down on our food expenses wasn't the agony and deprivation we had feared it would be. In fact, by the end of March, we both agreed that this whole FIRE lifestyle thing was actually way easier than we anticipated. We were biking on weekends, eating leftovers for lunch, and having friends over to the house. And now that we'd tackled the small stuff, we knew it was time to make bigger changes.

CHAPTER 5

BMWS AND BOAT CLUBS

The "BMW saga" — as it came to be known between Taylor and me — started long before I heard about FIRE. It actually started with the birth of Jovie. Before then, Taylor had been driving a 2010 Chevy Equinox. It was a reliable car, but Taylor and I had both gotten into the habit of upgrading our cars after a few years. Now, of course, I think that makes absolutely no sense. Why give up something that isn't broken? Most cars can easily last fifteen or twenty years, so why stop driving one that's only four or five years old? But at the time, we didn't question this kind of thinking. We had justifications: *We need a four-wheel drive for our trips to Tahoe. When a car has over a hundred thousand miles on it, I don't trust it on the freeway. I want a new navigation system. I want a sunroof.* The truth was: We liked to drive nice, new cars.

So I wasn't surprised when, a few months after Jovie was born, Taylor mentioned wanting a new car. I had recently upgraded to a newer Mazda, whose $250 monthly lease payment seemed like a steal. But I was surprised when she said she wanted a BMW. I didn't think of us as flashy, image-obsessed BMW people. I pictured us as sporty and practical Mazda or Subaru drivers. But Taylor was firm: She wanted a BMW.

We agreed that the most we could afford was a $400 monthly payment. She could have a BMW if she found a lease that low, but I was pretty confident there wasn't a BMW dealership anywhere in the state that would give her that kind of deal. I was hoping she would get so frustrated with the search for a BMW that she would come home with a more reasonable (and affordable) car like a midsize SUV to make loading and unloading Jovie easier.

A week later, Taylor pulled into the driveway in a black 2015 BMW 3 Series GT Hatchback, a stunning race car. BMW is one of the few manufacturers that offers leases on used cars, and Taylor happened to find an older BMW with a $2,000-down lease and a $401 monthly payment. I learned a valuable lesson that day: My wife can overcome almost any obstacle, no matter how improbable the odds, with a smile on her face.

Nevertheless, after making our commitment to a more frugal lifestyle, I thought it was obvious that the BMW would be the first luxury to get rid of. Taylor, however, had made it clear from the first moment I mentioned FIRE that the BMW was nonnegotiable. Since then, she'd refused to discuss it. If I wanted to keep my wife on board with FIRE, I was forbidden from mentioning those three letters.

■ ■ ■ ■

I knew that if I had any hope of getting Taylor to reconsider her BMW decision, I needed to make a painful decision of my own and cancel my boat club membership. I needed to show her that I had skin in the game, that I was willing to sacrifice something that brought me great joy for the benefit of the family and for FIRE.

When Taylor and I first moved to the San Diego area, our plan was to spend lots of time on the water — surfing, paddleboarding, kayaking, and swimming — but that didn't happen. We were working so much we never had time to do any of those things. I'd dreamed of owning my own boat, but this dream had been crushed by the reality that I didn't have the time to maintain one, never mind the $500-per-month slip fees. ·

When I made my pitch for the boat club membership, I told Taylor: "Every morning, I drive across the Coronado Bridge and look out at the beautiful ocean, and I'm reminded what I'm missing. This is driving me crazy. If I'm going to work this hard, let's make it worth it."

The particular boat club I wanted to join allows members to pull up, get out of their cars, and literally walk onto a boat that fits their needs — whether to take friends out for a sunset cruise or to fish for yellowtail off the nine-mile bank. Then, after a day or evening on the water, members can dock the boat, hop off, and head to their cars. No maintenance, no cleaning, no time wasted. All you have to do is cover gas when you use the boat. Plus, you can use the affiliated clubs all over the country! At the time, this was perfect for us, a busy, traveling family who wanted the joys of boating without the burdens of boat ownership.

And I was right: The boat membership was amazing. I took my clients out on the bay, Taylor and I brought Jovie out for picnics, and I spent evenings fishing with buddies. It was some of the best money I'd ever spent on myself, and I honestly couldn't imagine giving it up. But with FIRE, every expense had to be put on the chopping block. The frustrating part was that I'd already sunk $6,000 to pay for the initial membership, which was a one-time cost in addition to the monthly fee. If I walked away from my membership, that was wasted money. Economists call this the "sunk cost fallacy."

DEFINITION: THE SUNK COST FALLACY

The "sunk cost fallacy" is a common misconception for people new to the FIRE journey. People want to spend less on gas, but they don't want to sell their gas-guzzling truck because of how much it has depreciated. Or people want to move to a smaller and cheaper apartment, but they refuse to move because they just bought new furniture that wouldn't fit in a smaller apartment. Maybe you have a $200 jacket hanging in your closet that doesn't fit you anymore, and you can't bear to get rid of it because of how much you spent on it.

The sunk cost fallacy is what happens when you assign value to an item based on money that you've already spent but that is not reflected in the item's actual market value or what it will be worth in the future. Basically, that investment is gone, so don't factor it in when making a decision about keeping or getting rid of something. Your jacket's value isn't $200; it's whatever you can get at the consignment store.

Put more simply, it means cut your losses.

Beyond helping me recognize sunk costs, the FIRE framework provided a powerful decision point for any outlier purchase: *Do I want this boat club, BMW, gym accessory, or drone, or do I want to be financially independent in ten years? Is this item or service a priority for my life and my happiness, and if so, is it more important than becoming financially independent within our target date?*

On a gorgeous Saturday in early April, about five weeks after Taylor and I had first started our FIRE journey, I took the family out on the water one last time. It was a beautiful

San Diego afternoon, 72 degrees and sunny. We hopped on a twenty-foot Hurricane Bowrider at the Cabrillo Isle Marina and cruised out into San Diego Bay. Taylor and I popped a couple of our favorite local beers and toasted to the good times we'd had on the bay. As the sun was setting, we passed the *USS Midway* Museum and the handsome downtown skyline. Watching Tay chasing Jovie across the back deck, I thought that while I was going to miss this experience, it would be worth it if I could have more time with my family. At least, I hoped so.

■ ■ ■ ■

"Honey." I took a deep breath. "We need to talk about the BMW."

I'd canceled my boat club membership the week before, and since then, I had been nervous to bring up the BMW. But I knew I couldn't put it off any longer. Even after canceling the boat membership, slashing our entire entertainment budget, and giving up our Amazon addiction, our average expenses were still over $8,000 a month. I wanted us to become a one-car household; to do this, I planned to bike to work instead of driving. Since we were only spending $250 on the lease for the Mazda, it made sense that we would ditch the BMW and its $400 monthly payment.

Taylor was not thrilled that I was bringing up the BMW again, but when I promised that I wouldn't push her to make any decision she didn't want to, she agreed to at least discuss it. Vicki Robin, one of the pioneers of FIRE, cowrote in her book *Your Money or Your Life* that you should evaluate your purchases by comparing the fulfillment they will (or do) provide with the amount of time you have to work in order to afford them. How much of your life is each purchase worth? Taylor agreed with this approach, so I pointed out that most of the "value" of a luxury sports car is in the Gran Turismo engine, but Taylor wasn't using the turbo features. Taylor replied that she really loved driving the BMW. It was important to her and brought her happiness, and she was willing to compromise on every other expense to keep it.

To me, keeping the BMW went against all the FIRE principles, so even knowing how strongly Taylor felt about it, I couldn't let the topic go. Finally, I asked her, "Honey, what's going on here? You've never been a big car person, and now you're hanging on to a powerful engine and leather seats like it's your life calling. This doesn't seem like you."

"Look," she said, "I work hard, and I spend most of my time stressed and tired. I don't get to be with Jovie full-time like I want. We aren't swimming in money at the end of the month. I need to justify it somehow. I need to feel that it's all for a good reason. When I see the BMW, I can see why I'm working so hard, and I get to enjoy that little victory."

I understood what she meant. I'd felt that way so many times when I bought myself a new phone or an expensive concert ticket. But all these luxuries added up, and the cost was years of our life committed to working these purchases off. I knew what I had to do — I pulled out the retirement calculator and showed her what keeping the BMW meant to our retirement date: If we kept the BMW at an annual expense of $4,812 (the exact lease was $401 a month), and added it to our annual budgeted spending of $60,000, our FIRE date was going to be extended by eighteen months. That was a year and a half spent away from Jovie, a year and a half of having to sit in meetings, on conference calls, or in traffic. Even leather seats couldn't justify a year and a half of our lives.

Taylor was speechless.

"Are you sure the math is right?" she asked me.

Here are the numbers I showed her:

RETIREMENT TIMELINE WITHOUT THE BMW

YOU CAN RETIRE IN **11 YEARS**
WITH A SAVINGS RATE OF **58%**
ANNUAL EXPENSES 60,000
ANNUAL SAVINGS 82,000
MONTHLY EXPENSES 5,000
MONTHLY SAVINGS 6,833

RETIREMENT TIMELINE WITH THE BMW

YOU CAN RETIRE IN **12.5 YEARS**
WITH A SAVINGS RATE OF **54%**
ANNUAL EXPENSES 64,812
ANNUAL SAVINGS 77,188
MONTHLY EXPENSES 5,401
MONTHLY SAVINGS 6,432

Within a few days, Taylor posted the car to swapalease
.com. It took a few months for us to find somebody to take
over the lease, but eventually we did, and when the day came,
we both watched as the man drove the BMW out of our driveway and out of our lives. For months after, Taylor and I talked
about how much she loved that car and missed driving it, but
she always said that once she understood how much time it
was costing her, she didn't regret giving it up. I was amazed to
watch this transformation in her. This really hit me whenever

we explained our new lifestyle to someone we'd just met, and Taylor would offer up the BMW story as an example of the choices we were making and the impacts they had on our future. At first, I had felt so lonely in this pursuit. I was anxious that I would be the one always saying no or questioning expenses; I didn't want to become "Scott the fun hater." And here she was, only a few months later, excitedly sharing the story of losing her BMW for a cause she believed in.

This is a story I have heard over and over on our FI journey: Sometimes people give up luxuries they actively enjoy, even every day. Maybe a lake house or a personal trainer or a house with a swimming pool. But when faced with the realities of how long they will have to work to pay for that luxury, they gladly decide (sooner or later) to give it up.

It has also become clear to me that our possessions are so much more than just objects. They have meaning in our lives — the same way my boat club membership represented the outdoorsy life I wanted to live and the way Taylor's BMW was a token of all she was working for. The night we let go of the car, Taylor turned to me and said, "When I saw that guy driving my car away, it made me so sad. But it wasn't about the car; it was about me. It was like a part of 'old me' was leaving."

I understood perfectly. In the past, when Taylor and I spent a couple of hundred dollars on a sushi date, or I bought a roof rack for the Mazda so we could carry the surfboards, it felt like symbols of the successful, fun-loving life we were living and the couple we wanted to be.

Now I see our decisions in an entirely new way. By not spending on those experiences or items, we put our long-term happiness ahead of short-term enjoyment. The hard part is staying the course.

FIRE VEHICLE GUIDE

Like most purchases in the financial independence community, there is a FIRE-approved method to buying a car, a tried-and-true process that combines self-reflection, cash, and data.

This doesn't mean you have to follow these guidelines or make the same choices. Plenty of people on the FIRE path are two-car households, drive newer cars, or even stick with their gas-guzzlers. As long as you're making an intentional choice to optimize your happiness, you do you. (But please consider eco-friendly options. You know you should, and our children will thank you.)

Self-reflection: The first step is to be honest about what kind of car you actually need. Which features feel necessary and which features are just for fun? You might find that you need a much simpler or smaller car than you thought. That annual trip to Home Depot can be done in a rented or borrowed truck. How often will you use a sunroof? Or a turbo engine?

Cash: Avoiding a loan or lease and buying a car with cash does two things: It lowers costs (since loans and leases add thousands in interest and additional costs), and it gives you bargaining power. It also opens the door to buying a car from a private party free from the hassle of trying to get financing.

Data: As Mr. Money Mustache points out in his article "Top 10 Cars for Smart People," most people use anecdotal information to decide about a car. They have one friend whose Kia broke down, so they won't buy Kias, and so on. "The key to finding a reliable car is to throw away all the anecdotal personal stories that you might have heard, and look to a source that actually collects this data from thousands of people."

Pursuing FIRE in the Big City

By the Numbers

Pre-FI career: Sales
Current age: 32
Projected age at FI: 40
Current annual spending: $110,000

What FIRE Means to Me

To me, FIRE means having the option to wake up in the morning and make the day my own. I want a simpler life. More time for my family, hobbies, a bit of nature, and the option to do nothing. Weekends are awesome. Who doesn't like the weekend? I want to create a lifestyle where every day feels like a weekend.

My Path to FIRE

My wife, Charlotte, and I graduated during the 2008 recession, and our combined annual earnings were $52,000. We both were pursuing historically low-paying fields (sports and arts) and had never focused on high-earning jobs because we were "following our passions." We both quickly realized that meant working jobs that demanded time away from friends and family and didn't give much in return. After a few years, we both pivoted to careers that offered better work-life balance.

Fast-forward a few years. As we progressed in our careers and started earning more, I wanted to figure out how to best use this newfound income. Stumbling around online, I came across the FIRE wormhole and got sucked in. When I first heard about the concept of FIRE, it seemed absolutely ludicrous. How can anyone earning a "normal" income afford to retire before sixty-five? When I took an afternoon to sit down and look at the numbers for the first time, I was amazed to realize that despite all the specifics of our situation (high-cost-of-living area, multiple children), on paper, this concept seemed possible.

In a Nutshell

- ✓ After graduating, we earned salaries of $27,000 and $25,000 at the start of the recession in 2008.
- ✓ When we discovered the FI concept at twenty-nine, our net worth was $170,000; three years later, dozens of tiny changes have allowed us to increase our net worth to $570,000.
- ✓ We have been intentional with major life decisions (buying cars, buying a house, getting married, having children) — each of these were expected events that we didn't jump into until we were ready, both emotionally and financially.
- ✓ We live a normal life; we simply aim to be conscious of the things we spend our money on — we ask the questions, "Does it add value? Does it make us happier?"

The Hardest Part

The hardest part of pursuing FIRE for me is that it's a somewhat lonely path in the day-to-day "real" world. Speaking openly about finances is taboo, and even among close friends it's a challenging topic to broach. It's hard not to be evangelical about the FIRE concept, but most attempts to bring it up with friends lead to a discussion of why their particular circumstances make it too challenging.

The Best Part

Now that we're several years into the journey, our FIRE plan has fully materialized and is actually working. While the end result will be rewarding, I take great pride and enjoyment in keeping the plan in motion. FIRE is a marathon. If I can do this, I genuinely feel like anything in the rest of my life is possible. It's the ultimate empowerment move.

My Advice to You

For traditional employment, don't pursue your passion. Find a company that appreciates its employees and will provide challenging work for equitable compensation. Make the rest of your life about pursuing your passions.

CHAPTER 6

GOODBYE, CORONADO

On August 8, 2017, five months and twenty-six days after the morning when I first heard about FIRE, I was once again driving over the Coronado Bridge. But this time, instead of heading to another day at the office, Taylor and I were leaving Coronado for good.

■ ■ ■ ■

The decision to leave California happened fast, but for years I had been feeling that California had gone from being our dream life to the thing standing between us and our long-term goals. It wasn't until FIRE that it became clear we would have a much richer (in every sense of the word) life somewhere else.

Canceling the boat club membership and getting rid of the BMW erased our hesitation to make big changes. We went through the house looking for things we could sell on Craigslist or eBay. We brainstormed ways we could reduce the $2,500 monthly cost of Jovie's childcare, like switching her to a daycare that would save us $700 a month. But we kept coming back to the same idea: It was damn expensive to live in Coronado, and if we could cut our living costs across the board, things would accelerate at the same pace as our growing impatience with anything spendy.

This wasn't our first foray into trying to find a more affordable living situation. In early 2015, a few years after we moved to California and long before we heard of FIRE, Taylor and I decided to seriously shop for a house. House prices were rising fast, and interest rates were at an all-time low. Everyone was telling us to get in the real estate game. We knew we wanted to have a child, and we knew our 650-square-foot, one-bedroom rental in Coronado, though perfect for two people, was too small for raising a family. Besides, isn't that what adults do? Hadn't we arrived at the "Buy a House" item on the to-do list of a "normal American family"?

We started by looking at houses in Coronado. One-bedroom condos cost around $700,000. Even with our healthy salaries, it didn't seem possible to save for the down payment we'd need, let alone get approved for that big a mortgage. (Surprisingly, we got close. We learned it's a mistake to equate what someone will lend you with what you should actually spend!) Everything else in Coronado was just as expensive, and the nearby beach towns of Carlsbad and Encinitas were almost as bad: Condos there started at around $600,000.

"We'll just move farther east into San Diego," I told Taylor. "We'll only be a few miles from Coronado, and we'll be able to get a much more affordable house."

This proved wildly inaccurate. We wanted to stay below $500,000, but we quickly found that meant moving far away from friends and the ocean and adding a very long commute. It was pretty discouraging. Eventually, we found a listing for an attached townhome that was fairly close to our $500,000 budget, and the real estate agent promised it was within walking distance of the beach. We arrived to find it at the intersection of two busy roads, and getting to the beach meant passing under a six-lane freeway. The carpet and paint hadn't been updated since before the internet existed, and the living room bore the scars of wild parties and keg stands. It was basically a bachelor pad for surfer dudes who didn't care about noise, traffic, air quality, or even laundry, apparently. And it could be ours, all for the low price of $500,000!

We weren't opposed to getting our hands dirty, and we even considered making an offer, but it didn't matter anyway. The place got five cash offers the next day. In fact, during our real estate adventure that year, we put in roughly ten offers, all over asking, and never had a single offer accepted. At one point, we lost our minds and offered $680,000 for a house, just to see what would happen. We didn't get it. So we gave up trying to buy and eventually, when Jovie was born later that year, we simply rented a bigger, three-bedroom place.

However, now that we were striving for financial independence, we reconsidered homeownership. After all, if we were going to spend $3,000 a month to live, why throw away that money on a rental? We started combing through Zillow like it was our full-time job, and we widened our search to towns and neighborhoods in California we had never imagined living in before. We compromised on a yard, square footage, safety, schools, anything short of running water! And we lowered our budget: Instead of spending $500,000, we wanted a home for no more than $400,000. We played with the idea of buying a duplex; we'd live in one of the units and rent out the other. We talked about renting an extra bedroom to a roommate or to Airbnb travelers. Maybe we'd downsize and move back into an apartment.

Then one day I started looking at other areas of the country, including my hometown in Iowa. I knew it was cheaper, but I didn't realize how much: Taylor and I could buy a four-bedroom house in the place I'd grown up for around $150,000. That sounded more like the people I had been reading about: FIRE converts who lived in low-cost rural areas and smaller Midwest towns. It made sense: Career opportunity was one of the biggest benefits of living in a larger city, and once someone reached financial independence, they wouldn't need that benefit. Plus, the prevalence of remote work opportunities means it's never been easier to earn a big-city salary while living in a cheaper location. I sent Taylor a link to an article about the cities with the lowest cost of living in the country. "Anything look good?" I asked her. No reply. Instead, Taylor sent me links to rundown apartments in California for $400,000, and I replied with links to beautiful modern $400,000 homes in other cities. As with the BMW, we reached another standstill. Taylor wasn't budging on her desire to stay in California, and I started to believe that a half-million-dollar dilapidated shack was in our future.

DOES FIRE MEAN YOU HAVE TO LIVE SOMEWHERE CHEAP?

When I started writing this book, I assumed you had to live somewhere cheap to achieve FIRE. Thankfully, I've since met many people who show that it's possible to achieve FIRE wherever you live. The key is *how* you live. Sure, the big costs of housing and childcare are much higher in the big city. But as Liz Thames from the popular blog *Frugalwoods* explained to me, certain advantages to urban life — public transportation, walkable neighborhoods, cheap groceries, free entertainment — can help to counterbalance those costs, depending on your priorities.

I still think pursuing FIRE is much harder if you live someplace with a high cost of living. You'll definitely have to say no to many concerts, dinners out, and other expensive fun times that might divert your attention from your newly frugal ways. In our experience, we paid enormously to live in Coronado without enough clear benefits (besides being near the beach). Our jobs, families, and interests were all available to us in other places. But if you don't have the luxury of being able to move or to work remotely, don't worry. The good news is that it's totally possible for you to pursue FIRE wherever you live.

I'm guessing Taylor and I would still be struggling over San Diego real estate if I hadn't gotten the crazy idea to film a documentary about FIRE. It all started in March 2017. I was talking with a client about how documentaries are such a powerful way to spread a big, bold idea, and I listed all the documentaries that had really *affected* me — *Minimalism*, *180° South*, *An Inconvenient Truth* — and even the experience of making my own documentary in 2014, *Inventing to Nowhere*. All of a sudden, a light went on for me. After I hung up, I googled "financial independence documentary" and found a thread on Reddit titled "Documentaries relevant to FIRE." But the only films mentioned were *Minimalism* and a short film called *Slomo*, about a doctor who quits his job to roller-skate. I found some documentaries dealing with similar themes, like tiny housing or the retirement crisis, but nothing specific to the FIRE movement.

This really surprised me. I knew *Mr. Money Mustache* had reached more than twenty-three million people. And there are nearly 400,000 people on the Financial Independence subreddit as of this writing. This was clearly a growing movement, so why was there no feature film that captured its message? I immediately started dreaming of directing and producing a documentary about FIRE. After all, I was excited about the concept, and the majority of my career involved video production. I imagined flying around the country interviewing all these people I was reading about: Mr. Money Mustache, the Mad Fientist, the Frugalwoods, Vicki Robin, and so on.

However, I knew this was probably unrealistic, and the documentary idea might have stayed in my head if it weren't for a lunch I had a few weeks later with my mother-in-law, Jan. She's an inspiring business owner and successful entrepreneur, and over beers, I found myself unloading about how stuck I felt and how much I resented working for somebody else.

"Why did you take the job?" she asked me.

I reviewed what had happened: how my video business had shuttered because of my partners, so I had taken a job in a creative agency to provide a steady source of income, which Taylor and I couldn't be without, both because of Jovie and because of Coronado's high cost of living. Yet I was starting to realize how much my identity was tied up in being a successful business owner. Without that role, I was struggling to remember who I was.

Then, in the middle of a packed brewery in downtown San Diego, sitting across from my mother-in-law, I started crying. I tried to blink the tears away, but they just kept coming.

"I think I'm really unhappy," I told her. I had everything I could have asked for — a healthy child, a wonderful marriage, a senior role in a growing company — but I felt so trapped. I didn't want to admit it. I felt like I had gotten myself into this mess, and it was my job to fix it, but the truth was, I was miserable and I needed advice.

Jan reached across the table and squeezed my wrist. "Finish your beer," she said. "I'm going to pay the tab, and then we're going for a walk."

During our walk, I told Jan about FIRE and how we were trying to change our lifestyle, but that every year only brought new and more overwhelming expenses. I told her how much I wanted to get back to a simpler life, with less stress and more time with my family. I mentioned my dream of making a FIRE documentary, which I couldn't stop thinking about.

Finally, she turned to me and said, "Scott, here's what I don't understand. If you want to quit your job and do this film, what are you waiting for?"

I knew what I was waiting for: permission. It was time to talk to Taylor about quitting my job.

■ ■ ■ ■

When I told Taylor everything I'd told her mother, she was not as surprised as I thought she'd be. As it turned out, she had noticed how detached and uninspired I had been acting. She later told me that ever since I had shut down my business, I had been walking around with a dark cloud over my head. The secret I thought I had been guarding so carefully was clearly yesterday's news. She said that if quitting my job and taking freelance work so that I could pursue this documentary would make me happy, she totally supported the decision. Then I casually mentioned the idea I'd been toying with: What if I quit my job and we left California and traveled around the country for a year? We could visit and stay with friends and family while I filmed the FIRE documentary, which would save a big chunk of money on rent and childcare (since I and our parents could watch Jovie). Taylor could keep working her job remotely, and along the way, we might find a less-expensive city to live in, one we loved as much as Coronado. I'm not going to lie: Taylor was much less enthusiastic about the idea of traveling and moving, but she agreed to think about it.

In late April, after a couple of weeks of discussion, Taylor and I were biking to the Coronado public pool with Jovie for "swim lessons," which meant holding our one-and-a-half-year-old toddler in the water while she splashed. It was a perfect California spring morning. Smelling the ocean breeze, I admired the town we'd lived in for years and come to love. Maybe staying wouldn't be so bad, I thought to myself. We would have to work longer to achieve FIRE, but maybe I'd find a way to worry less and enjoy the weather. Just then, Taylor looked over at me and said, "I think I'm ready to move."

I almost fell off my bike. What had just happened?! Taylor explained she had been thinking about how much she loved biking with me and Jovie and having time to relax. If moving gave her more free time and meant she could stop working a few years earlier, she was game. Besides, her job let her work from anywhere, and my job was making me unhappy. She also realized that if we traveled the country while still working, we'd be able to save a lot of money along the way. This same epiphany is what had led her to decide to get rid of the BMW.

As soon as we got back home, I ran the numbers based on staying with friends and family and living in some long-term rentals. Assuming Taylor kept working and I brought in money by freelancing, if we traveled for twelve months we would be able to save $50,000 in one year! That was more money than Taylor and I had saved in any five-year period of our lives! And it would be enough for us to make a down payment on a new home.

■ ■ ■ ■

Once Taylor agreed to the idea of a yearlong trip, our plans fell into place fast. We sat down and came up with a list of prerequisites for our dream city to settle in after our travels: It had to have a low or reasonable cost of living; be near a large airport; have plenty of sunshine (preferably high-desert climate); have a population between 100,000 and 250,000, or big enough to have jobs, culture, and growth but small enough to feel connected; have good schools; and be within a half-hour drive of lots of outdoor activities. Finally, because of Taylor's job, it had to be located west of the Mississippi. After much deliberation, we narrowed the choice to this short list of places:

Bend, Oregon
Fort Collins, Colorado
Boise, Idaho
Spokane, Washington

Next, we had to talk to our landlord. We were only six months into a two-year lease on our place, so if we couldn't break the lease, we would have to rethink our road trip. We expected our landlord to be upset, and we practiced what we were going to say. Then we invited her over for a glass of wine and told her the whole plan: about FIRE, about the trip and the documentary, about how this felt like the smartest way for us to spend more time with our daughter. We promised to help her find new tenants, even to get her more rent (as we knew we had scored a deal). Then we waited. Would she agree? Or would she tell us we couldn't break the lease?

Amazingly, she was actually more interested in hearing about FIRE than in talking about the lease. After asking us a bunch of questions, she said, "You need to do this. Don't worry about the house." It felt like a miracle. This was the first time (but not the last) that we saw how strongly the ideas behind FIRE — taking back your time, being with your family, finding meaning in your life — resonate with people, no matter what their financial circumstances may be.

Later, as we were getting ready for bed, Taylor looked over and said, "We're really doing this, aren't we?" Something about getting our landlord's blessing made the whole decision very real. I didn't want to admit it to Taylor, since my obsession with FIRE had started us on this path, but I was terrified. We'd been on a lot of adventures together in our marriage, but never anything like this. Taylor and I loved San Diego; we had built a life here. We had friends, a professional network. Our baby was born here. And what if it didn't work out? What if it made us miserable, defeating the purpose?

The final step was deciding on a departure date. I was eager to get started — in part, so we didn't get cold feet — so I suggested June 15, about five weeks away. Taylor felt that was moving a little too fast and suggested January 1, eight months away. "I'm not sure I can wait that long," I admitted.

"It's already agonizing to sit and wait, plus every month is so much more time before retirement. Now that we've decided to go, I want to take the leap before we lose momentum." We agreed to compromise and set our official departure date as August 1, 2017.

SCOTT & TAYLOR'S TRAVEL PLAN

We wanted our yearlong trip to be a mix of seeing family and friends, exploring new cities, and having fun. Taking a year off to drive around the country felt like a rare opportunity, and we wanted to make the most of it while also getting serious about finding our new home. We also wanted to leave some of our trip unplanned so that we could be spontaneous. Here's what we originally came up with:

Early June 2017 — Visit friends in Spokane, WA.

August — Leave San Diego! Drive to Seattle to stay with Taylor's family. See Bend on the way.

September — Live rent-free in Seattle at Taylor's parents' home.

October to December — Live rent-free in Iowa at Scott's parents' home.

October — Go to Ecuador for Chautauqua (a financial independence retreat).

Mid-December — Go back to Seattle for Christmas with Taylor's parents.

January 2018 — Rent for a month in Boise, ID.

February — Rent for a month in Bend, OR.

March — Rent for a month in Fort Collins, CO.

April to June — House-sit in Hawaii.

July — Buy and settle into our new home in our new city.

It took a few weeks to finalize our travel plans, but by early June all that was left was telling our friends and packing our house. As we'd soon learn, different people react very differently to the idea of frugal living and retiring early. When we announced to everyone what we were doing, most of our friends were really supportive, but some were skeptical about the FIRE concept, some thought we were crazy to leave beautiful Coronado, and some expressed envy that I was pursuing a creative project and ditching my nine-to-five job. Many friends shared their own challenges with trying to save money while living in such an expensive place, and everyone offered a friend or relative for us to see or stay with on our travels. Of course, not everyone we knew was interested in living a FIRE lifestyle, but it felt good to have the support of our community.

When I turned in my notice at work, my boss asked if I'd be willing to address our small team at a weekly meeting and let them know that I was leaving and why. It was a nerve-racking moment because it was one of the first times I had to stand up in front of a group of people and articulate this project and the FIRE principles behind it. I imagined my coworkers laughing at my project or rolling their eyes at the idea of quitting my job and moving my entire family over a half-baked scheme. But overall, the feedback was positive. A few days later, a coworker even told me that she'd been having a similar thought of quitting her job to start her own venture and that she was going to see if living more frugally might make that happen faster.

Packing our house was yet another reminder of how far removed our lives had become from the FIRE ideals. We donated or sold so much stuff that we'd bought just the year before. We found a few brand-new items in the garage with the tags still attached: Why did we need two ladders? Or three different fancy wine openers? Or eight martini glasses we'd never used? We'd bought so much unnecessary stuff for Jovie. All of this made me realize that I didn't want to be a mindless consumer anymore. I wanted my time and my money to actually *mean* something. We packed all the household items we were keeping into a storage pod (I ordered the smallest option — 16'x 8'x 8' — as a challenge to ensure we downsized), and we packed all our necessities into our car. Whatever we couldn't fit into the pod or the car was sold or given away, and I promised myself that the next time we settled into a home, I wouldn't fill it with unneeded stuff.

As our departure date came closer, I could tell that Taylor was getting more and more upset at the thought of leaving California. I kept reassuring her that this would be the adventure of a lifetime, that all we had to do was have a great time seeing our families and checking out new cities, and then we'd have the money to buy a house.

■ ■ ■ ■

Moving wasn't the only thing that was happening quickly. The documentary was gaining steam fast, due in part to a voicemail I left for the duo who run the *ChooseFI* podcast, Jonathan and Brad. Here's what I said:

> I wanted to reach out to you. I am actually hoping to spend the next year or so creating a documentary about FIRE and the community that has really transformed my life. I believe it has the power to transform a lot of things in this country and even the world.

Amazingly enough, they mentioned the documentary project during a podcast episode, and overnight my inbox filled with emails from the FIRE community. People had suggestions and ideas, they wanted to share their stories and tips, and they wanted me to know how excited they were that I was doing this. The reaction gave me unexpected momentum and helped me secure an investor, someone who was as passionate about

FIRE as I was. This funding allowed me to get serious about planning the film. I needed to secure a production crew, create a budget and timeline, and decide what "story" I would tell. I needed interviews with folks in the FIRE community, and I needed access to and the cooperation of those people. I've learned that some people are excited to participate in a documentary, but for others, it's a nightmare. I was optimistic that things would work out, but there was a long road ahead.

Most of all, our plans sounded cool on paper — this year on the road was shaping up to be a genuine, once-in-a-lifetime opportunity — but could we actually pull it off? How would we travel, keep working our jobs, film a documentary, look for a new hometown, and save money, all at the same time? How were we going to care for and raise a two-year-old while moving constantly? How would we handle leaving behind our routines, our friends, and our comforts, while living with our parents for the first time in over a decade? There were lots of positives I was looking forward to, but I worried that Taylor would blame me if this entire idea turned out to be a disaster. And why wouldn't she? I had been the person pushing for FIRE since I'd heard about it. If all this fell apart, I would be responsible.

■ ■ ■ ■

Our final night in San Diego, we hosted a beach bonfire to say goodbye to our friends. It was also our first night of filming, so I was running around trying to finish packing, grab firewood, and still arrive early to meet the crew and help them set up. At first, I felt incredibly awkward in front of the camera. I've been involved in film for over a decade, but mainly on the production side, and here I was, essentially interviewing myself and others while trying to act natural and get all the shots we'd planned. *Have we covered our feelings of guilt, of sadness, of fear? Will it feel contrived? Do my friends find this odd?* Soon, though, as the discussion flowed, my worries, along with the cameras and crew, faded into the background.

Later, after we wrapped shooting, I sat drinking a beer and looking around at all the amazing people we'd met in California. Before coming to Coronado, Taylor and I had never lived anywhere for so long. We'd gotten married here, had our baby here, built careers here. I looked out at the waves crashing on the beach and thought about all the weekends we'd spent sailing, surfing, and swimming in these waters. Were we ever going to find a place as beautiful as this? Was there any city in the world that could compare? Suddenly, everything felt overwhelmingly real and rushed. I was overcome with a mixture of sadness, excitement, and fear. Tomorrow morning, we were leaving, not to a new career or similar life, but to something completely different. Something that I didn't know how to articulate. All I knew was that our life in Coronado, no matter how wonderful it was, wasn't the life I was meant to live. So we were throwing ourselves into the unknown, hoping that wherever we landed, we'd find a home, a community, and a new direction. But there was no turning back now. After all, that would be too expensive. No doubt about it, we were playing with FIRE.

TAYLOR'S TAKE: LEAVING CORONADO

Leaving Coronado was one of the hardest things I've ever done. I had always assumed that we'd raise Jovie there and even grow old there — it was our home! So when we drove away for the last time, it was heartbreaking. I think I was probably silent for two days of driving, just thinking about how many amazing friends we'd made in Coronado and how painful it was to leave.

Every time Scott and I have made a big change, I've worried that we will regret it. When we left Reno, I worried that we wouldn't like San Diego. When we moved out of our condo, I worried that we'd miss living in such a small space together. And every time, I've ended up being happy that we made the change. That's what I told myself as we drove over the Coronado Bridge for the last time, that whatever was waiting for us was going to be even more amazing.

THE JOURNEY BEGINS

CHAPTER 7

"This place is heaven on earth." When Taylor uttered these words, we were halfway through a walk around Mirror Pond in the middle of Drake Park in downtown Bend, Oregon. Beautiful ponderosa pines stretched up toward the bluest sky in every direction. The only sounds we could hear were the birds in the branches, the wind blowing through the trees, and kids playing nearby. Snow-covered mountaintops were just down the road.

At this point, we had driven through San Luis Obispo, Healdsburg, Arcata, and Klamath Falls on our way to Bend. The built-up desert landscape of Southern California had turned into the striking beauty of Northern California, and later, the solitude and dense forest of Oregon. Now we were on the last stretch of our trip before hitting Taylor's hometown, Seattle. Bend was the first on our list of potential new hometowns.

"This feels like a different planet…is this real life?" Taylor said. It really did — the perfect planet for an FI lifestyle. Bend fit most of our criteria: Water and mountains were nearby, along with miles of trails, world-class fly-fishing, and even waves to surf…in the river! Nice three-bedroom houses ran about $350,000. The school districts got high marks. The airport flew directly to seven major cities. You couldn't throw a rock without hitting a recycling bin or solar panel. Bumper stickers demanded "Be nice. You're in Bend."

In the past, Taylor and I had considered where to live based on career potential and our vision of "paradise": tropical weather, palm trees, white sands, and so on. Now I realized how much we had taken for granted in Coronado and how false our assumptions were. The truth was, in order to be happy, the small things made the biggest difference — living within walking distance of grocery stores, being able to bike wherever we needed to go, living in a community of friendly people who looked out for each other. I saw Bend through the lens of FIRE, and it felt right: Bike trails to save money on driving? Big backyards to play in? Cheap car insurance? Nearby camping? No sales tax? Free concerts, festivals, and farmers markets every weekend? These things would have a huge impact not only on how much money we could save but on our happiness.

Then some friends told us that their grandparents, who lived in Bend, would be traveling from January to March. They would happily let us stay in their beautiful home for a ridiculously low rent, but only if we committed to all three months. According to our travel schedule, that would mean scrapping our plans to visit Boise in January and Fort Collins in March. Shouldn't we at least check out those towns? After discussing it, we decided that Boise was too far from Taylor's parents, and Fort Collins was too far from an airport. Taylor reminded me that we had intentionally decided to be flexible with our travel plans, in case we unexpectedly fell in love with a place. We just hadn't thought it would happen in the first city we visited! With that, we made a plan to come back and give Bend a proper three-month test drive, and we continued our journey to Seattle.

■ ■ ■ ■

If you ever want to feel like you've made the biggest mistake of your life, do the following: Decide you want to change your life completely, convince your wife to cut expenses by 50 percent and give up her dream car, quit your job, and move your family a thousand miles to live with your in-laws.

As we drove closer to Seattle, and the glow of Bend wore off, all I could think about was how I was going to explain our plan to Taylor's parents, who must have been convinced their daughter had married the wrong guy. Sure, Jan was the one who'd encouraged me to quit my job and pursue the documentary but I still worried about how our families were going to react to our unconventional new life. Would they take it as a criticism of their lifestyle choices? Would they be as excited about FIRE as we were?

Despite my worries Jan and Gary welcomed us warmly when we arrived, and after all the chaos of moving and of anticipating this major life change, it felt amazing to settle into a home, even if it wasn't our home. If Taylor's parents thought we were crazy, they didn't mention it, and we spent the first week relaxing, catching up, and spending time with Jovie.

Those first couple of weeks of our trip felt like my first chance to relax in months, years even. Instead of taking a seven-day vacation from work and feeling like I had to squeeze every last drop of fun out of it, I knew that this was going to be my new normal. I wasn't going back to a job anytime soon. That freedom also gave me the chance to spend more time thinking about my documentary. Having made a documentary before, I knew how much time, money, and planning they took, and while I had an investor and had gotten filming under way, I had an insane amount of work to do.

One night in Seattle, we made plans to have dinner with some close childhood friends of Taylor's, Jennie and her husband, Nick. We were particularly excited to talk to them about FIRE. They had a much more mature relationship with money than we'd ever had. They were painstakingly frugal and had a well-baked plan for their future. Even when we'd gone on weekend trips together in the past, they always put financial decisions through the "Is it in the budget?" filter, which we perceived as them being "cheap." Now we'd come full circle —

we had a budget! We were being frugal! As Taylor joked, "We could have learned so much from them, but now we get the chance to admit how much we got wrong about money and their approach to it and hug it all out."

After dinner, Nick started the money conversation by asking, "So, tell us about this FIRE thing."

Taylor and I gave them the overview of FIRE and why we thought it made sense for us. Hearing Taylor promote FIRE to other people was the highlight of my evening. Ever since we'd made the decision to move, I couldn't help worrying that she was doing this for me, that deep down she wasn't onboard with this lifestyle change. Hearing my wife fully embrace the principles and even explain the math behind FIRE helped ease my doubts.

"What's the plan now?" Jennie asked in her usual reserved way, but I could tell she wasn't sold on the idea.

We talked them through our big adventure, and I mentioned that a key aspect of cutting our expenses was using geo-arbitrage, the concept of relocating in order to take advantage of the lower cost of living in other places. For us, this meant staying with Taylor's parents for a couple of months, staying with my parents in Iowa for a couple of months, and then (per our revised plan) living cheaply in Bend for a few months to see if it was a good fit as our new hometown.

"It just seems like this geo-arbitrage thing involves living with your parents for free. How is that being financially independent?" Nick said. I felt myself get defensive and start backpedaling. We weren't freeloading, or not entirely; staying with our parents also gave Jovie some rare extended time with her grandparents. Plus, four months of free rent wasn't going to make us financially independent. It was a chance to save some extra money before relocating to someplace cheaper than Coronado, where we'd establish our new FIRE-friendly lifestyle.

"But what exactly are you going to do when you don't have to work?" Jennie asked. "I don't know. Who are these FIRE people? It sounds a bit like a cult."

We were stunned. We thought Jennie and Nick, of all our friends, would understand best, and we even thought they might want to join us! But it was clear they didn't trust this vision of FIRE or its goals. Eventually, we had to change the subject, but the air stayed thick with tension the rest of the night. On the drive home, Taylor said she felt like a total idiot and never wanted to talk to anyone about FIRE again. I agreed with her: Why did FIRE make so much sense to us but not to most of the other people in our lives?

DEFINITION: GEO-ARBITRAGE

Geo-arbitrage, a term made popular by Tim Ferriss, refers to using geography to lower your expenses. Most of us practice geo-arbitrage in our lives, whether or not we're aware of it. It might be as simple as moving to a cheaper area of town so you can have a bigger house, or vacationing in Mexico and not Hawaii because it's a cheaper way to visit the beach. Other forms of geo-arbitrage include going to Thailand for dental surgery because the procedure is $6,000 cheaper there than in the United States, or working remotely for an NYC company (and making an NYC salary) while living in rural Pennsylvania. Or moving to a state with no state income tax (like Washington or Florida) or no sales tax (like Oregon or Montana) to take advantage of the savings. You might say, geo-arbitrage simply means taking advantage of the different costs of the same goods and services in different locations.

The next morning, I received an email from Kalen, a woman who had heard about the documentary on the *ChooseFI* podcast. In the past year, she and her boyfriend had committed fully to a life of FIRE: They had sold their cars, maxed out their retirement accounts, and were saving 65 percent of their income (see her "FIRE Story" at the end of this chapter). She wrote: "I can't express how life-changing the realization that I don't have to work until the age of sixty-five has been for me. I see the pursuit of financial independence as a way to get in touch with the important things in life and truly as a cure for a certain brand of millennial depression."

Yes, I thought. *This is why we are doing this! This is the whole point!* And in terms of "a certain brand of millennial depression," I knew exactly what she meant. Millennials have been stuck with seemingly insurmountable student debt, shaky job prospects, a planet that's falling apart, whiplashing politicians calling for the privatization of Social Security, and the end of pensions. I read the email to Taylor, and it made us realize: Maybe we just needed to find our people, the ones who were on this path with us and could cheerlead us along the way.

We'd learned our lesson, though. We needed to tread carefully with people who were new to the FIRE lifestyle. We also wondered: Did some people react negatively because they felt judged? Did they think we were looking down on them if they had a big house or a new car? "Of course we aren't!" Taylor said. "That was us a few months ago!" In addition, not everyone liked the idea of retirement as a goal. Like me, a lot of people had their identity so wrapped up in their work that they couldn't imagine their life without it. Whatever the reason, we decided that in the future, we would be careful not to overwhelm people with our enthusiasm. We'd wait to see if they were interested before we started to share. Clearly, this was a more sensitive topic than we had anticipated.

■ ■ ■ ■

Our stay in Seattle included two of the biggest highlights of our entire yearlong FIRE journey. The first highlight came in the form of an email from Travis Shakespeare, a senior vice president at BBC Worldwide who had heard me on the *ChooseFI* podcast. He was a FIRE convert who was based in LA but would be traveling through Seattle the following week. He asked to meet, get a beer, and talk about my project. Instantly, I was nervous. What did that mean? Was BBC interested in my documentary? Were they already working on something? The only way to find out was to go meet him.

We met at a dim sum restaurant and immediately connected over our love of food and our experiences working in production. Travis was likable, curious, and warm, and after an hour, I felt like we'd been friends for years. Eventually, Travis cut to the chase: For a couple of years, he'd been planning to do a documentary about FIRE, and when he heard me on the podcast, he was upset that he hadn't moved faster on his idea. But after thinking about it, he realized that the reason he hadn't taken action was that he didn't have a specific story or a "hero" to root for. Now he felt like Taylor's and my journey of discovery would be the perfect linear narrative to take the audience along for the ride and naturally introduce the experts and influencers who helped create the FIRE community. However, he saw an issue with my plans: that I couldn't effectively be both the director and the main character. In short, he wanted to direct my film.

I was speechless. This was equal parts a dream come true and my biggest fear. To have a director with his level of experience and industry connections meant that this film had a much greater chance of making an impact. Just the fact that he wanted to work on it with me was hugely validating. But if he was going to direct my film, that meant I had to give up creative control of my project. Most importantly, this would be a serious partnership, and I had just met this guy. What if it turned out he was crazy, and then I was stuck with him? Or what if we had completely different ideas for the film? I told him I was interested, but I needed to think about it. On the drive back to Taylor's parents', I called her and just kept saying, "Holy shit! Holy shit! Holy shit!" Everything was happening so fast and in ways I'd never imagined.

The next day, I called Travis and told him I would be honored to work together. Ultimately, having Travis as the director of *Playing with FIRE* felt like an opportunity I couldn't turn down. It was a leap of faith, but I knew if I was serious about this film and about accomplishing my mission of spreading FIRE to others, Travis had the vision to make that happen. I had to put my ego aside and do what was right for the project.

As Travis and I worked out the details of our partnership (which included getting written permission from the BBC), I also partnered with a video production crew out of Portland called Only Today. Ray, Zippy, and the rest of the Only Today team were old friends of mine and a joy to work with. They had won multiple prime-time Emmy Awards, and we had even partnered on a few projects in the past. Only Today would handle all things technical on set, including producing, location scouting, principal photography, audio, and DIT (or handling captured footage). I felt confident they would be able to execute this production on the highest level, and just as importantly, they expressed a genuine interest in FIRE and its potential to improve people's lives.

■ ■ ■ ■

The second highlight of our trip was the chance to meet Vicki Robin, the coauthor of *Your Money or Your Life*. Although first published in 1992, this book is still considered one of the most pivotal and impactful books in the FIRE community. Basically, I was starstruck when it came to Vicki, a woman who had been living our new lifestyle for over three decades and knew the joys and pitfalls better than anyone. I knew she lived in the Pacific Northwest, and I'd emailed her a few weeks before we left on our trip and asked if she'd be willing to be interviewed for my FIRE documentary.

While we were in Seattle, I got a reply — Vicki lived on nearby Whidbey Island, and to my utter delight, she said yes and invited me to take the ferry to meet her. I couldn't pack the car fast enough. And as further confirmation that Taylor and I were full partners in our future, Taylor said there was no way she was going to let me meet Vicki by myself. I joked that she'd come a long way from ignoring my crazy emails full of links to FIRE articles, but it meant a lot to me.

Taylor and I, along with the documentary crew, caught a ferry at the Mukilteo Terminal north of Seattle and rode across Puget Sound, with the Olympic Mountains peering up on the horizon, to Whidbey Island. A striking, confident woman in her seventies with hawklike eyes and a big smile, Vicki was authentically friendly and a joy to be with, as were so many of the people we would meet on this journey.

Over lunch, the documentary crew rolled while Vicki told us about her story — how she left a traditional path to pursue a completely uncharted life. "I sacrificed a normal life with normal rewards and normal relationships for something that was off-the-charts weird. I graduated college realizing that the whole journey of academics and success and being the president of this and that and the other thing was so empty.... I didn't even know how to boil water! I didn't know how to live. I had not been prepared for life. I had been prepared for being a very narrow-focused person who would rise to the top as some professional and have enough money to pay everybody else to do the rest of my life."

Instead, right after college, Vicki took a small inheritance, invested it in Canadian bonds, and turned that into a lifetime of passive income. She used that money to travel the world, live in a bus, build a yurt, survive winter in the backwoods of Wisconsin, and ultimately start teaching a finance framework with her partner, Joe Dominguez, which they turned into the internationally bestselling book *Your Money or Your Life*. A week after its initial publication, Vicki appeared on *The Oprah Winfrey Show* to promote it, and Oprah told her audience: "This is a wonderful book. It can really change your life." The next day, it became a *New York Times* bestseller, and it remained on the *Businessweek* bestseller list for five years. She has recently re-released an updated version that has earned high acclaim.

Taylor and I were amazed by Vicki's story, which reminded us of why we had started this journey and helped soothe any worries we'd started to have. Radical change isn't easy, and I often forgot that I hadn't even heard of FIRE a year ago. Yet here I was having lunch on a tiny island in Washington talking to the person who had revolutionized financial independence and, in many ways, started it all.

As we got ready to leave, Taylor asked Vicki if she could give us any advice. After all, she had seen hundreds of people walk the FIRE path. What pitfalls should we look out for? Vicki considered the question before replying: "My advice is to figure out what you really want to do with your life, figure out what's important to you, and intern yourself in those situations. FI is like heading toward a cliff, and if you don't learn to fly before you get to the edge of the cliff, you'll never jump."

On the ferry home, Taylor and I talked about what Vicki meant. Did we know what we really wanted to do with our lives? We'd both felt like we did, but now we were struggling to articulate it. I'd assumed I would just start some kind of entrepreneurial venture, but was that really what I wanted — to keep working? And if I already had enough money, what was the point of putting in so many hours on a business idea? Similarly, Taylor said that Vicki helped her realize that her goals weren't as simple as "stay home with Jovie." That might be enjoyable for a few years, but what about when Jovie was in school full-time? We had been so focused on getting to FIRE quickly that we hadn't spent a lot of time thinking about what life without a normal job would look like. We agreed that as soon as we were settled in our new home, we would start trying to figure out what we actually wanted to do with our lives so that we didn't end up standing on the edge of a cliff of our own making, too afraid to leap into our next adventure.

Is FIRE the Cure for a Certain Brand of Millennial Depression?

By the Numbers

Pre-FI careers: Management analyst, local government
Current ages: 26
Projected ages at FI: 32
Current annual combined spending: $32,000

What FIRE Means to Me

The realization that I don't have to work until the age of sixty-five has been life-changing. I see the pursuit of financial independence as a vehicle to get in touch with the important things, bringing clarity to an often overwhelming and confusing world. For me the idea of financial independence is a cure for my millennial depression — a term to describe the general mood I found myself in after arriving in the postacademic "real world," looking ahead toward decades of working a nine-to-five job and thinking *Is this it?*

My Path to FIRE

My boyfriend, Kyle, and I were introduced to FIRE when Kyle's mom told us about Mr. Money Mustache and JL Collins. I was becoming interested in investing and she, having casually followed these blogs for years, thought they might be a good starting point. Kyle was already into biking and being frugal, but he wasn't optimizing his money through investing. I was more of an unconscious spender. I experienced a turning point while describing my wanderlust to Kyle — I had this desire to pick up and move to a new city, not wanting to be "tied down" to a specific job and place. The realist to my idealist, he challenged me by asking, "With what money?" It sounds simple, but this was the first time I realized that money equals freedom and possibility.

Once we discovered the online FIRE community, our lifestyle changed rapidly. We began tracking our spending, focusing on saving, and contributing to tax-advantaged accounts. We also sold two trucks and put that money into taxable investments, downsizing to one Toyota Camry. In addition, we traded an unnecessary car commute for the daily joys of walking.

The big decisions — to sell the cars, to maximize retirement savings — were intimidating at first, but we've never looked back. Our relationship with money has changed completely. Instead of spending unconsciously and finding ourselves stressed with piles of material things we don't need, we've begun to see money as a tool to fund our long-term goals. We're realistic about allowing those goals to change as we do. Once you experience the paradigm shift of conscious spending, it's hard to go back.

In a Nutshell

- ✓ In 2016, we started tracking our spending, investing, maxing out IRAs and 401ks, and so on.
- ✓ We currently save an average of 65 percent of our income.
- ✓ We live in Kyle's house, which he bought in 2010.

The Hardest Part

When we started this journey we were each making under $50,000 a year, which was intimidating because many people in the FIRE community are in higher-earning brackets. When you're middle-income or lower, some of the traditional advice doesn't apply. Still, we didn't let this discourage us. Once we started saving and investing we realized how rich we were — it's all relative to your lifestyle. Those interested in financial independence shouldn't let their salary deter them from saving as much as they can.

The Best Part

The biggest positive has been the consciousness shift in our lives. Once we woke up to the fact that external symbols of success like career, car, and house weren't important to us, a new world of possibilities opened up. All of a sudden, time seemed more valuable and we became pickier about how to spend it. Instead of buying meaningless items and fleeting experiences, we try to fill our time with simple and cheap pleasures like taking walks, reading books, bonding with our pets, and engaging with friends and family.

My Advice to You

Don't inflate your lifestyle; save as much as you can. Redefine what success means to you.

CHAPTER 8

WHAT THE HECK IS AN INDEX FUND?

Our meeting with Vicki made one thing starkly clear: We couldn't achieve FIRE and change our lives on our own. We needed help from people who were in the process of reaching or had already reached financial independence. This was about emotional support as much as practical advice. Although we wanted to find a balance with our non-FIRE friends, we had felt resistance and tension. When we talked to FIRE people, we felt excitement and received motivation.

Fortunately, more good fortune was in store for us. In September, while we were still in Seattle, I decided to email Pete Adeney, a.k.a. Mr. Money Mustache himself. He'd recently announced that he was opening a coworking space in his hometown of Longmont, Colorado. I wanted to feature Pete in the documentary, and the grand opening of his new place would be the ideal event; it would also be a perfect opportunity to meet Pete and get to know other Mustachians. As incentive, I offered to create a promo reel of the grand opening that Pete could put on his website. He agreed, so I flew to Colorado with my video crew to meet my new hero and the man who had (unknowingly) changed the course of my family's life forever.

On the way, I thought about what I would say during our interview. Should I tell Pete that I had quit my job just a couple of months after hearing him on a podcast? Would that be weird? Would I like him? Would we have anything to talk about? Was I just another fan-guy obsessed with meeting an idol? Naw, that wasn't me...or was it?

Mr. Money Mustache World Headquarters, as it is called, is

located in a nondescript building in the middle of downtown, with a pawn shop on one side and a charming soap and ceramics shop on the other. When I arrived, as far as I could tell, the building was empty except for a guy on a ladder with a screwdriver, who nodded at me as I came in. I mumbled something about looking for Pete. Did people call him Pete? Should I call him Mr. MM?

All of a sudden, Pete peeked around the corner.

"Hey," he said, "you must be Scott."

I introduced myself and the crew. I felt like a ten-year-old at Comiskey Park meeting White Sox Hall of Famer Frank Thomas during warm-ups. After a little chitchat, he motioned to a broom in the corner and asked if I wanted to help sweep. Then he started hooking up a keg.

I'd attended grand openings and met "big-name" celebrities in the past, and this was nothing like that. There was no big ego or polished script, no managers, assistants, or PR teams. Pete clearly wasn't trying to impress me or make me a fan, but he also wasn't treating me like a groupie. He was just Pete, a fortysomething guy making his own baseboard to install a tap system to pour local brews to share with his friends. *Wow,* I thought. *Is this the mecca of life-changing inspiration I was looking for? Did I expect Mustachianism to be anything else? What was I expecting?*

Over the next few hours, I helped Pete sweep the back patio, wash off chairs, and dust the custom bookshelves he had built by hand, and I even poured a delicious local Left Hand Brewing Company pilsner from Pete's new handmade tap system. The crew filmed as the room went from empty to packed, and Mustachians of all kinds filled the modestly furnished and hand-built work space. The grand opening of Pete's space was also a potluck, so people walked in the door with a bike helmet in one hand and a casserole dish in the other. Conversations sprang up about how to install DIY solar panels, the math behind income properties, the Tesla Model 3, and the best way to repair your old winter coat. It wasn't long before all my previous anxiety melted away. Who were these amazing people?!

After spending months immersed in "Mustachian lore," I shouldn't have been shocked, but I was! I loved the intentional way each person approached their life. Everyone had thought long and carefully about how they wanted to spend their time, what kind of house would make them happiest, how their values aligned with their spending, and what was most important to them in life. This was a happy, welcoming, and optimistic bunch.

True to his low-profile philosophy, Pete didn't kick off the night with a big speech or a toast. He just grabbed a glass, filled it with beer, and started talking to people. Similarly, at the end of the night, there was no grand closing statement or announcement. I'm not even sure if there was a tour. When the event was winding down, people just picked up their bike helmets and empty dishes and headed out. This was something about Pete that I would continue to learn over the next few months: He did what he wanted. He could not be persuaded, pressured, or sweet-talked into anything he didn't want to do, whether that was giving an interview to a high-profile publication or spending thirty dollars on a Kobe burger. As one of his friends put it that night, "It doesn't matter if there's a hundred-thousand-dollar deal waiting on Pete. If his son wants to go to the waterpark, he's gone."

I flew back to Seattle the next day renewed in my passion for FIRE and smiling on the inside just knowing that somewhere in Colorado was a building full of people who were so open to welcoming a newbie like me into their community.

■ ■ ■ ■

In October, we left Taylor's parents and flew to Iowa to drop Jovie off with my parents. Then Taylor and I got back on a plane and flew to Ecuador for a financial independence retreat with some of the most innovative and well-known minds in the personal finance world.

The original reason we had booked the trip was to film interviews for the documentary. Unfortunately, the event organizers felt it would be too intrusive to have a film crew at the retreat, so we had to scrap that plan. However, the trip was a great way to meet more of the FIRE community (and enjoy some international travel). I was also looking forward to spending some time with Taylor that wasn't interrupted by our work: she had been dealing with a hectic month in her job, and I had been running around like crazy trying to juggle my freelance work and the documentary.

Founded in 2013 by JL Collins of jlcollinsnh.com (famous in the FI community for his amazing Stock Series and his book, *The Simple Path to Wealth*), FI Chautauquas have now been hosted in Ecuador, the UK, and Greece. JL's vision was to bring together some of the leaders of the FI community and invite a small group of his readers and listeners to enjoy a week of adventure and conversation about life, freedom, happiness, and investing. Our fellow attendees came from far and wide and included a Mustachian who worked at Google, a nurse and her husband who wrote a blog about their FIRE journey, another couple from San Diego, and a Chilean coming all the way from Dubai, to name a few!

It was surreal to be surrounded by so many of the FIRE characters who had influenced me and Taylor to make this enormous transition in our lives — such as Pete, Paula Pant (the brain behind the popular blog and podcast *Afford Anything*), Chad Carson (a successful real estate investor who blogs at *Coach Carson*), and Brandon Ganch (the blogger and podcaster at *Mad Fientist*). However, the key person we would learn from in Ecuador was JL.

■ ■ ■ ■

Until FIRE, I was terrified of investing. I had always watched my parents play it safe with money, and I had followed suit without even questioning their approach. For years I told myself that I just didn't have enough time to learn how to invest "the right way," so my best bet was to avoid investing entirely. I put 10 percent of my income into my retirement accounts, checked the balance every year, and forgot about it. However, even though I didn't *really* know the difference between a stock and a bond, I convinced myself I probably knew more than most of my friends, and later, I told myself that I *was* investing — in my business. *Who needs the stock market when you have your own equity to build?*

By this time in our yearlong FIRE journey, Taylor and I had a jumble of accounts that totaled $216,000: We had saved $54,000 in cash (in checking accounts); we had recently invested $23,000 in a taxable brokerage account at Vanguard; and we had $139,000 in six different (tax-deferred) retirement accounts, which Taylor and I had collected over the years. Why had we chosen particular funds? No idea. We both felt completely clueless about how to invest.

All that changed in Ecuador when we met JL Collins. Many of the FIRE influencers have become known for specialties: Mr. Money Mustache for low-cost living, the Mad Fientist for tax optimization, and JL as the FIRE community's go-to for investment and stock advice. On his blog, *The Simple Path to Wealth*, JL has a "Stock Series," which currently includes thirty-plus posts that distill his advice on investing and personal finance, which are also available in his book, *The Simple Path to Wealth: Your Road Map to Financial Independence and a Rich, Free Life*. JL's writing style is very approachable and fun, and he makes investing easy to understand; his work is also backed by many decades of experience and research.

According to JL, I didn't need to spend hours researching

portfolios and stocks and checking on the market and trying to predict what would happen or understand what it all meant. His simple path to wealth is just this: Spend less than you earn, and invest the balance in index funds.

If you're anything like me, when someone mentions something like "index fund investing," you nod your head knowingly and let the conversation move on to something you understand, too embarrassed to ask the obvious question: "What's index fund investing?" As I researched FIRE, at least four people separately recommended index funds to me, including Mad Fientist's Brandon Ganch during Chautauqua, and each time, I kept quiet, reluctant to admit how little I actually knew. JL fixed that. Here is what I learned:

THE BASICS OF FIRE-APPROVED INVESTING

1. Index Funds Are Awesome

An index fund allows you to invest in the stock market without buying individual stocks and without trying to understand, play, or "beat" the stock market. An index fund uses computer algorithms to buy up whole baskets of stocks that mimic and represent the entirety of the stock market. Throughout history, on average and over the long term, the stock market overall has gone up approximately 10 percent per year; thus an index fund that reflects the market will most likely experience a similarly positive, predictable result.

Stock index funds are low cost, and they are a central component of the FIRE playbook. They are the universally accepted and most popular investment choice in the mainstream FIRE blogosphere. That said, the number-one fan of index funds is arguably Warren Buffett, the chairman and CEO of one of the world's largest companies, Berkshire Hathaway. Buffett is usually found in the top three of the wealthiest people in the world, and he is considered by many to be the world's best investor. He's jolly, folksy, down-to-earth, and generally beloved. Even though he oversees an enterprise with almost 300,000 employees, his office has only twenty-five employees. He doesn't own a computer; he lives in his first home, which he purchased for about $50,000 in 1958; and he usually eats McDonald's for breakfast. He himself points out that beyond the use of a private jet, his lifestyle greatly mirrors that of the average upper-middle-class American.

For decades, Warren Buffett has consistently and unequivocally recommended low-cost stock index funds for the average investor. When he was recently asked how he would invest his first million dollars if he could start all over again, Buffett laughed and said, "I'd put it all in a low-cost index fund that tracks the S&P 500 and get back to work."

In his 2014 bestseller *Money: Master the Game*, Tony Robbins describes how he tried to interview Warren Buffett but was steadily rebuffed. Buffett told him, "Tony, I'd love to help you, but I'm afraid I've already said everything a person can say on the subject." But, Tony persisted, "what kind of portfolio would you recommend for your family to protect and grow their own investments?" Buffett smiled and grabbed Tony's arm. "It's so simple. Indexing is the way to go. Invest in great American businesses without paying all the fees of a mutual fund manager and hang on to those companies, and you will win over the long term."

I WANT TO INVEST. WHAT DO I DO NEXT?

If you've set up an investment account before, you probably know how simple it is. But if not and/or if you're like me, the process of setting up the account can feel intimidating and can be a reason to put off investing. You might not be ready to invest yet, but setting up the account is still an important first step and Vanguard allows you to fund your account at a later date. Here are the steps to follow to open a Vanguard account:

1. Go to personal.vanguard.com and click, "Open Your Account." You'll be asked if you're opening a new account or moving an outside account, and their system will guide you through the process from there. If you'd prefer to open your account over the phone, call 877-320-3099 and one of their advisers will walk you through it.

2. It's time to pick your funds! Most FIRE bloggers recommend VTSAX, which is an index fund that represents the entire US stock market. VTSAX has a $10,000 minimum investment, but they have a similar fund called VTSMX that has a $3,000 minimum investment. There are also great index fund options without any minimum investment.

2. Avoid Money Managers (or Be Prepared to Pay)

As it turns out, trying to beat the performance of the stock market statistically doesn't work. Only 15 percent of professionals manage to beat it, and what's the likelihood that the person you've hired is one of those 15 percent? Not very high.

Because an index fund doesn't require a building full of portfolio managers, analysts, and traders to work diligently day in and day out to try to beat the stock market, indexing is dirt cheap: the expense ratio of the Vanguard index fund VTSAX, a FIRE favorite, was 0.04% when this book went to press. Meanwhile, the typical human-managed mutual funds typically charge 1 to 2 percent per year.

In the past, that mutual fund cost didn't ring alarm bells for me. A percent or two seemed like a perfectly reasonable amount of money to spend on someone helping me manage my money. Then I heard Brad Barrett of the *ChooseFI* podcast talk through a calculation. He explained that if you started with $100,000 and invested that in a low-cost index fund for forty years at an expense ratio of 0.05 percent with an expected return of 8 percent, you would have $2.13 million dollars. With a money manager investing that same money in the same scenario at around 1 percent, you would end up with $1.4 million dollars. You would lose $630,000 to someone who was not doing a thing different than what your low-cost index fund could do for you.

So why doesn't everyone invest in index funds? I don't know. Maybe, like me and Taylor, people think they're doing the right thing just by contributing to their 401ks and by hiring somebody to help them invest, not realizing that they're actually shooting themselves in the foot. As JL told us, no one will take care of your money better than you.

WHAT IF I DON'T WANT TO MANAGE MY OWN INVESTMENTS?

In the beginning, Taylor and I weren't sure that we wanted to manage our own investment accounts. Especially while we were both working and trying to spend as much time with Jovie as possible, becoming our own investment advisers didn't seem like a good use of our time. This is something I hear frequently: "I want to invest, but I don't have the bandwidth or interest to do it myself." Remember, the most important thing is that you get started and that you're aware of your options. Working with your current bank or hiring a fee-only adviser might be the easiest, most accessible way to get started and that's fine. As long as you know what it's costing you and you're making an intentional choice based on your lifestyle values, you're on the right path to intentional investing. If you're looking for a financial adviser, the National Association of Personal Finance Advisors can point you in the right direction.

3. Compound Interest Is the Most Amazing Thing Ever

As with index funds, I had a basic understanding of compound interest, but until I talked with JL, I just nodded along without fully appreciating what it would mean for my bank account. Here's how it works: Compound interest basically means getting interest on interest. Or, to put it differently, you achieve compound interest on your investments when you don't spend any of the interest those investments earn but instead add them to your original investment. Thus, if you invest $100,000 with a 10 percent rate of return, this will earn $10,000 in interest after a year. If you add that to your original investment, you'll have $110,000. Next year, 10 percent interest on $110,000 will earn $11,000, and if you combine it, you'll have $121,000. Here's what happens over decades.

Age of investment	Value of initial $100,000 investment with simple 10% interest	Value of initial $100,000 investment with compound 10% interest
1 year	$110,000	$110,000
3 years	$130,000	$133,100
5 years	$150,000	$161,051
10 years	$200,000	$259,374
20 years	$300,000	$672,749

The idea is that your money earns money, and the money your money earns also earns money, and so on, and so on, and the difference after decades becomes exponential.

■ ■ ■ ■

After talking to JL, Taylor and I took a walk around the retreat center's garden. We talked about our money education up to this point in our lives. Taylor had learned about investing from her dad, who had instilled a healthy fear of debt and taught her the "set it and forget it" approach to investing. Not bad advice! In my family, we hadn't discussed investing at all. I knew that my mom handled my parents' investments, but that was it. Taylor and I were both told, "Don't go into credit card debt, invest in your 401k, and you'll be fine," and we had followed that to a tee. The end result was that we had put minimal amounts of money into our 401ks and then passively attended to those investments and missed out on over a decade of meaningful financial growth.

What could we do about it now?

I was torn. Part of me felt that we should give up the idea of buying a house and just put our $50,000 into index funds immediately. Another part knew I would be happier using, and growing, our money by investing in a business.

Taylor said that part of her struggle with our FIRE journey was that she could feel all the negatives (giving up her car, living with family, eating at home), but she couldn't feel the positives (a higher net worth, more cash). It was just money on a screen to her.

We made a tentative decision to split our portfolio three ways: Invest 33 percent in index funds, 33 percent in real estate, and 33 percent in our own business ventures. As it turned out, over the next few months, we revisited this conversation and decision over a dozen times, both with each other and with others. We found that most people on the FIRE path are constantly reevaluating the ways they are investing their money. Brandon Ganch told us that, after having a negative experience with being a homeowner, he mainly invested in index funds. Paula Pant talked about how she felt comfortable having a large portion of her net worth in real estate because of how well she understood it. During our conversation on Whidbey Island with Vicki Robin, she talked about using her wealth to create more wealth for others (while also providing an income) through local micro-loans. It amazed me (and continues to amaze me) how much opportunity for good there is for a conscious and intentional investor.

TAYLOR'S TAKE:
LET'S TALK ABOUT INVESTING!

Before we started this journey, I could probably count on one hand the number of times I'd talked about investing. It just wasn't something that crossed my mind. Whenever I got a new job, I would sign up for the 401k, pick a fund at random, and never think about it again. It amazes me to realize that for most of my life investing never came up in conversation, I had no idea how my friends or family handled their investments, and it didn't even occur to me that I was missing out on something incredible. Now I talk about investing to anyone who will listen! Especially as a woman, I think it's important that I am educated about how my money is being managed. I want my daughter to feel empowered to handle her own finances.

Next, we wanted to learn about real estate investing. One of the speakers at this modern-day Chautauqua was Chad Carson, a real estate investor from South Carolina who blogs at

Coach Carson. Throughout our week in Ecuador, we kept getting drawn into fascinating discussions with him regarding his real estate, his life philosophy, and our shared love of sports, and he was happy to answer our questions: Is real estate investing smart? Is it safe? What advice did he have for total newbies?

Chad shared his own story with real estate: He had started knocking on doors as a college student, trying to find any homeowners who were looking to sell their property and would accept a discounted price for quick cash. He then turned around and passed the deal on to a real estate investor, while pocketing a small markup. Eventually he earned enough to buy his own investment property. Now he and his wife owned over ninety properties in his hometown in South Carolina, and he had recently decided to move to Ecuador for a year so that his young daughters could become fluent in Spanish.

I asked what his secret to success was, and he answered immediately, "Frugality, persistence, and a thirst for learning." He had always lived on much less than he earned, and for years he had happily driven an old Toyota, even when he was making well over six figures and making over fifty real estate deals a year. That frugality helped him survive the 2008 recession and meant he always had cash socked away when a good deal popped up. Hearing him talk about his car made me think again about my Mazda, which for years I had thought of as my compromise car. Now it seemed like a luxury that was tying up precious resources. With all these opportunities to invest, as long as we had extra money, I could feel myself losing interest in sunroofs, navigation systems, and leather seats.

Over the years, I've met many brilliant and bold entrepreneurs. People who aren't afraid of big ideas. People who are willing to risk it all for the chance to build something world-changing. I've always loved being around that kind of energy and vision, so it was no surprise that I felt a deep connection to Chad. I admired him and felt like I understood him:

Like me, he was someone who had always resisted working for somebody else. Doing his own thing was the only way.

But among all these entrepreneurs, I noticed a striking difference between those who were driven by FIRE and those who were not: The former were on the path to (or had found) financial independence, and frugality was their superpower. They weren't afraid to take risks because they were hedging their bets with high savings rates and realistic money management. I now saw why I was so drawn to FIRE — I wanted to get the positives of entrepreneurship and creative projects without the stress of having to make them pay the bills. What could I create if I didn't have to worry about making a certain profit? I didn't know the answer, but the question itself filled me with excitement.

■ ■ ■ ■

The entire week of the Chautauqua, I was nagged by an unsettling thought: Though I was having a life-changing experience, everything I was learning was available for free on the internet. Did I really need to be here?

Before we'd left the United States, Taylor and I had gotten the same reaction from family and friends: *Why spend thousands of dollars to go on an international retreat to learn about not spending money? That doesn't seem very frugal. Are you joining a cult?* I had to admit, these were fair questions, ones I couldn't adequately answer. Why would someone on the path to FIRE spend that kind of money to learn more about FIRE? Further, what was the agenda of the organizers? Wasn't encouraging people to spend that kind of money leading them away from FIRE and a life of financial freedom?

All the retreat's teachers had been sharing their expertise for free for years on their websites, and I had read most of their material before landing in Ecuador. What difference would it make to meet these people in person? Why not apply the advice, save the cash, and reach FIRE?

By the retreat's end, I began to appreciate the importance of being there in person. For all my reading, I hadn't yet fully digested the FIRE concept, which I could now see that I'd been making more complex than it really was. I don't know if I would have realized this without the power of the conference's face-to-face guidance, in which experts talked to us about our specific situation. Not only was I understanding the simplicity of the "spend less than you earn and invest the difference" model, along with how to apply it in our actual lives, but I realized that we'd been doing it "right" since the start. If we stayed the course and kept learning, we'd reach FIRE.

Meeting people on a similar journey also turned out to be crucial. As much as FIRE is about saving money and financial freedom, it's about living a much calmer, more thoughtful, and self-directed life, and the experts I met embodied this. One memorable moment happened with Paula Pant. Paula's FIRE journey is fascinating: She went from being a newspaper journalist in Boulder, Colorado, to traveling around the world to buying real estate in Atlanta and starting an incredibly successful blog. Her motto is "You can afford anything, just not everything." In person, she is one of the calmest, most focused people I've ever spent time with. She has a low voice and doesn't speak much, but when she does, the entire room takes notice. One afternoon, she and I were sitting side by side on a gondola lift in Quito, and I was explaining that I was terrified of heights. Well, it didn't require much explaining — I was clinging to the side of the gondola and starting to hyperventilate.

"What helps me when I get anxious or scared," Paula said, "is knowing that I'm not in control of anything. When I truly accept that I have no control, I feel better."

Honestly, just listening to her speak made me feel better, but the sentiment blew my mind. A finance guru and real estate investor who accepts her lack of control? She was simply putting herself in the best position she could to achieve her goals. But she was cool with what she couldn't control. Damn. This group of FIRE experts wasn't just dispensing money hacks. They were showing us what intentional living looked like. They were leading by example, and witnessing this made a huge impact on Taylor's and my belief system.

In the past, Taylor and I would have had no qualms about dropping $5,000 on a vacation. In fact, on the flight back to Iowa, we talked about all the vacations we'd gone on where we'd gotten so much less than this one — to New Zealand to zip-line down the side of a mountain; to St. Thomas to lie on the beach. We've had plenty of fun and excitement but rarely experienced this deeper meaning, purpose, and connection. We both agreed that our time at Chautauqua included some of the most enlightening, deeply personal, and enjoyable conversations of our entire lives.

We also laughed at how misguided our expectations had been. We had thought it would be a true "financial conference" with boardrooms, fluorescent lighting, and PowerPoint presentations, and I had packed notepads and pens that had sat unused in our room. I also thought every conversation would be about investment strategies and money (nope). Obviously, as I've mentioned, people discussed investing, net worth, savings rates, and different strategies to spend less. But more often we focused on connection, happiness, and community, and Taylor and I loved it.

We were sad to leave our FIRE community in Ecuador. A world where it was completely normal for a conversation to cover weather, politics, reality TV, and the balance of your bank account. Where everyone laughed at the prospect of taking out a car loan or using your yearly bonus to buy a new TV. I found sharing our net worth, our entire financial picture, with near strangers to be incredibly liberating. I recommend it. It's especially fun when the reason for sharing is because you have a simple and exciting plan to retire early — not your average conversation starter.

Taylor and I realized that, moving forward, we would need to make our own world, one where we can live frugally but remain close to our friends who choose to live different lives. To us, FIRE isn't about judging the financial choices or priorities of others. It is simply a way to guide and judge our own decisions and priorities and to become more thoughtful and in control of our lives. Leaving Ecuador, we were more determined than ever to design a lifestyle that fit us and our new sensibilities and values. A lifestyle where we could focus on our baby, who was currently waiting for us in Iowa with my parents, a reminder of the reason we were on this adventure in the first place.

CHAPTER 9

GETTING SCHOOLED IN FIRE

We were back in Iowa for just a couple of weeks before another opportunity presented itself. Many of the FIRE bloggers we had just met during Chautauqua would be at FinCon, one of the largest personal finance media conferences in the world. Attended by over a thousand bloggers, writers, speakers, podcasters, and personal finance experts, FinCon was in Dallas that year, and if we got our film crew there, we could get a bunch of great interviews for the documentary, on a budget.

So once again, we said goodbye to Jovie and hit the road. All these trips — to Colorado, to Ecuador, and now to Dallas — were important, but the nonstop travel was exhausting. I missed the relaxed Saturday mornings we used to have in Coronado, drinking coffee with my wife and daughter on our porch.

Except for the many familiar faces, FinCon could not have been more different from Chautauqua. It was a typical large conference held in a giant convention center. On the first day, I walked the exhibit floor with Brad and Jonathan from the *ChooseFI* podcast, and I watched as fan after fan came up to them, telling them how the podcast had changed their lives. "FIRE is definitely much more of a topic this year than ever before," the event organizer, Philip Taylor, told me. It clearly was, and I felt honored to be a part of it. Just a few weeks after seeing Paula Pant in Ecuador, I hung out with her while she prepared to give one of the event's keynote speeches. Her topic? Forget what your audience wants and be authentic to your own voice because it's authenticity that will ultimately make you memorable. This resonated with me. Not everyone

I'd met thought my documentary was a good idea, and most people had strong opinions about how I should or shouldn't present FIRE. But ultimately I had to do what felt natural to me.

My personal highlight of FinCon was organizing a roundtable between some of the most influential FIRE voices: Carl Jensen from *1500 Days to Freedom*, Grant Sabatier from *Millennial Money*, Liz Thames from *Frugalwoods*, Tanja Hester from *Our Next Life*, Brandon Ganch from *Mad Fientist*, and J. D. Roth from *Get Rich Slowly*. First, everyone talked about how they had stumbled onto FIRE. Carl mentioned that, like me, he had found the *Mr. Money Mustache* blog, and it had instantly changed his life. Tanja found a book called *How to Retire Early* and used that as her blueprint. One thing everyone agreed on was that you don't need to be good at math to be good at FIRE. The math is easy; the lifestyle changes are hard.

From there, the group spoke about privilege. What did it mean to be talking about a lifestyle choice that for so many people feels out of reach? Liz pointed out that systemic barriers keep lots of people from even being able to consider FIRE: "If you don't learn financial literacy until late in life or never, I don't know how you're supposed to be able to do something like this." It was amazing to see this group of "money nerds" become so philosophical about the heart of the movement. I got chills and felt grateful to be part of this community and able, through the documentary, to amplify this conversation.

Another gift in Dallas was the chance to spend more time with Brandon. We had really bonded in Ecuador, and after the interview at FinCon, Taylor and I invited him over to our Airbnb for coffee. Brandon publishes some of the most current research related to tax code, retirement savings, and investing strategy. Taylor and I were hoping he could look at our jumble of numbers and help us come up with a more comprehensive plan for achieving FIRE.

Here is what he told us:

Brandon (Mad Fientist) kicked off by stressing how simple the FIRE concept is. He said it's important to not get obsessed with the details. The details are important, but the main thing is sticking to the basic formula: Spend less than you earn, and invest the difference. And the best way to get spending down? Focus on big-ticket items like cars and housing.

1. Spend Less Than You Earn

Brandon said that sometimes people confuse the saving and investing components of FIRE. Investing is, or can be, overwhelming, and people sometimes get distracted from what's actually important — which is how much they're saving. As long as you're saving, you're making progress, but the key to FIRE is saving money at a high or accelerated rate. Saving the most you can as quickly as you can is more crucial than investing those savings in a particular way. To illustrate, Brandon said that if Taylor and I could save 50 to 70 percent of our earnings and did nothing else other than stick it in a savings account, we would be fine and eventually achieve FIRE. He wasn't saying we shouldn't invest; he was just saying that saving money is the main focus.

Brandon went over our yearlong trip budget and found we were doing pretty well. Our planned budget was $4,200 a month (a shocking 55 percent reduction from our expenses in Coronado), but he thought there were ways we could be saving even more. Then, if we could maintain this budget in our new city, and we kept our earnings level around the same, we could be hitting 50 to 60 percent savings rates with relative ease.

In addition, Taylor and I had recently saved quite a bit already: We had started our trip with about $20,000 in cash, and we had been saving so much money over the past three months that we now had $54,000 in cash, which Brandon casually noted was enough to cover the costs of our yearlong trip: $54,000 divided by 12 (months) = $4,500 (per month). This was *more* than our budget. Obviously, we weren't going to increase our spending, but I was struck by this simple realization — we could stop working cold turkey for twelve months and cover our expenses with money left over. Talk about an antidote to our past paycheck-to-paycheck lifestyle! That we had already saved more money than we had ever saved before felt like one of the biggest "proof points" that we were benefiting from this FIRE experiment. And for the first time in my adult life, a unique feeling of freedom swept over me, one that sticks with me to this day.

2. Invest the Difference

Then Brandon discussed why investing is important. Basically, the key to FIRE is getting your money to work for you (versus you having to work for money). When your money is sitting in a bank account, it's actually losing value. Why? Because inflation increases at a higher rate than most bank accounts pay in interest. If that same amount of money was invested in the stock market, it would grow in value.

For example, in our situation, Brandon pointed out that we had too much cash. Having $54,000 might feel great, but our checking account was earning less than 0.1 percent interest. Brandon said we should take part of our accumulated cash and invest it in something that would earn from 5 to 10 percent interest.

Ahh, the highs and lows of the FIRE mentality. *Hooray, we're flush with cash! Boo, it's losing value due to inflation, so let's hurry up and invest it wisely.*

Our reasoning for not investing our stash of cash was threefold: (1) We were wary of stocks because they seemed so expensive and because, in 2017, we were in an unprecedentedly strong and long-lasting bull market; (2) we were saving for a down payment on a house; and (3) we were intrigued by the idea of buying a rental property.

Brandon explained that worrying about the risk and price

of stocks was a waste of time; historically, the stock market goes up over time, so buy stocks and keep them for the long haul. Buying and selling stocks based on short-term lows and highs, or trying to time the market, is an investing error to avoid.

"What's wrong with timing the market?" I asked.

"You'll lose," Brandon said. He said there were two options: We could just invest it all at once on a random day, or we could break it into smaller chunks and invest it at regular intervals (every month, for example). The first option was statistically more likely to earn us more, but the second option (which is called dollar cost averaging) might feel more comfortable to us as new investors. In this case, we decided that when we were ready, we'd invest $3,000. Because that wasn't enough to meet the $10,000 minimum of VTSAX, we would put the money in VTSMX, a similar fund with a $3,000 minimum. (For those of you with less than $3,000 to invest, check out VTI, which is another FIRE-approved fund without a minimum initial investment.)

DEFINITION: DOLLAR COST AVERAGING (DCA)

Dollar cost averaging is an investment technique that refers to buying a fixed dollar amount of a particular investment on a regular schedule, regardless of the share price. Over time, the highs and lows of the share price average out, which minimizes the risk of losing money. There are many opinions arguing for and against this strategy, but Taylor and I have found that it helped us overcome that initial resistance to putting our savings into the stock market. Our plan is to invest in increments of $3,000 over the next year. When we reach the $10,000 mark, Vanguard will automatically roll our investment into VTSAX.

Brandon did agree that planning to buy a house is a good (and necessary) reason to stockpile cash, and he also said that buying a rental property as a way of creating another stream of income can be a good way to invest.

ACCESSING RETIREMENT FUNDS EARLY

In Dallas, Brandon also answered a question that had been nagging me since we'd started our FIRE journey — why put so much money into retirement accounts if we can't access that money until we're fifty-nine and a half? This is something Brandon has researched extensively, so he was the right person to ask. He explained that, in addition to the tax benefits of these plans, there are various techniques for accessing that money before retirement without paying a penalty. One of the most popular techniques is a Roth conversion ladder, where you roll money from your 401k or other tax-deferred retirement accounts into an IRA and then withdraw it, tax-free. Other techniques include the Rule 72(t), which is an allowance from the IRS to withdraw a fixed amount of money from your retirement funds before retirement age and without paying the standard 10 percent penalty for early withdrawal (you still pay taxes on the funds; you just don't pay the penalty).

3. Focus on Your Car and Housing Budgets

During our hangout, Brandon called out the fact that we were still leasing a car — my 2016 Mazda 3. Lest he think I was just another thoughtless consumer, I explained the killer deal I'd negotiated: I was paying only $250 a month (for three years), and then I would be eligible to buy the car for a mere $12,300 (or less than the estimated worth of over $13,000 once the lease was up). What a steal!

Brandon was less than impressed. He suggested that we find a way out of the lease immediately, even if that cost a couple of thousand dollars, and then use cash to buy a car for around $5,000.

This was another example of the wide gap between being conventionally "good" with money and living the FIRE lifestyle. I had felt particularly proud of that lease negotiation, and even my family and friends agreed I had gotten a good deal.

But not Brandon. Not only would my car not be worth $13,000 by the time I bought it, but by first paying $250 a month for three years, I was essentially buying a brand-new car and just delaying the payment. A car is a depreciating asset, and mine was losing value daily. All told, I'd end up paying over $20,000 for a car that would steadily be worth less and less, until it "bottomed out" at a third or a quarter of its original value. When you're living a FIRE lifestyle, you want all your dollars working for you, and by definition, depreciating assets lose value or money over time. What's a depreciating asset? Almost any expensive object: diamond jewelry, boats, electronics, and of course, cars.

"But isn't that depreciation just the price of being a driver? I mean, we need a vehicle to get around in this world?" I asked.

Brandon explained that a car doesn't have to be a depreciating asset, or at least the depreciation doesn't have to be as severe! He said that the sweet spot for a car seems to be around $5,000. After hitting a certain point of depreciation, the rate at which a used car loses value slows down. You can get a reliable used vehicle with under 100,000 miles for this price, and if you don't drive it too much, that four-wheeled engineering marvel will get you from point A to B for at least another decade.

"What if we buy a $10,000 car?" Taylor pleaded. I knew she was picturing the soft leather seats of her long-gone BMW.

Brandon was unmoved. "Aim for $5,000."

Finally, Taylor and I talked with Brandon about the pros and cons of renting versus homeownership. This involves more than simply choosing the cheapest option. In Bend, we figured we could rent a three-bedroom house for around $2,000 per month, and we could buy a three-bedroom house for around $400,000. To decide which would be more economical, we had to run the numbers, since mortgages, interest rates, home values, and so on vary from market to market. For example, in Coronado, renting was our only viable option, since we couldn't afford to buy a million-dollar three-bedroom house. In Bend, it was a close call. Using the free "Buy vs. Rent" calculator offered by the *New York Times*, Brandon helped us find the answer to this question. The calculator told us that if we could rent for under $1,517, then renting would be more economical than buying a $400,000 home on a thirty-year loan. However, if renting in Bend cost at least $2,000 a month (which is what we expected), then buying the same-size home for $400,000 was the better decision.

Brandon stressed that we also had to consider our lifestyle and long-range plans. If you have your heart set on buying a forever home that you will grow old and die in, you should buy if you can make the numbers make sense in your budget. But if you hate maintenance or expect that you might move in the near future, renting might be a better fit, no matter what the numbers say.

Taylor and I both agreed that we wanted to own our own home. That was one reason we left Coronado in the first place. So we decided to keep our $54,000 in cash, so it would be available for a down payment as soon as we were settled. Brandon agreed with our decision, but he warned us that if we changed our mind about buying a house, we should invest some of that cash. Every minute it was sitting in a bank account, it was missing the chance to earn us money in the stock market.

How Hurricane Katrina Made Me Pursue Financial Independence

By the Numbers

Pre-FI career: Trial lawyer
Current age: 38
Age at FI: 32
Current annual spending: $20,000

What FIRE Means to Me

I graduated from law school in 2005 in New Orleans. I had just been offered a job at a firm. When the hurricane alert came through, I just took a change of clothes and my dog — nothing else. The building where I was supposed to start work was destroyed, and the firm told me that they couldn't hire me for six months. A week later, thanks to a citywide ordinance, my landlord told me I had three days to get out of my apartment if I wanted to be released from the lease. So I fit everything I could into my car and threw everything else away. Katrina showed me how little stuff mattered and how quickly everything you own can disappear.

My Path to FIRE

I have always been frugal, but I was completely oblivious to student debt, so when I graduated law school with $100,000 in student debt, I completely freaked out. I decided I was going to do everything possible to pay off that debt as quickly as I could. Even when I was working as a lawyer, I worked evenings and weekends as a delivery driver for Domino's. So people who knew me as a lawyer would order a pizza and then recognize me. I lived off the Domino's money, and my entire salary went to paying off my student debt. Then, as my career grew and my income grew, I still kept living frugally. That's the key: Keep your expenses low even as your salary grows.

It's been interesting being a single woman who is also financially independent. My idea of dating has been completely warped by FI because I don't want to go to fancy dinners or waste a lot of money dating. It's also made me much more judgmental about things in potential partners, like credit card debt and overspending.

In a Nutshell

- ✓ I became financially independent in 2012 with a fund of $1 million.
- ✓ I spend $50 a month on groceries and live in a 417-square-foot condo in Seattle.
- ✓ I'm still working. I run my own small law firm.

The Hardest Part

I think I overestimated what it would be like when there is no schedule, no deadline, no itinerary. That's part of the reason why I'm still working. Sometimes I'm worried that the idea of FI is better than FI itself.

The Best Part

I have more confidence in asking for what I want because if the answer is no, it doesn't affect my lifestyle. It makes me bolder in standing up for what I want. For example, I became self-employed because the law firm I worked for wouldn't allow me to make after-tax contributions to my 401k and couldn't offer me an HSA. I wouldn't have been able to take the risk of leaving my job if I wasn't FI.

My Advice to You

Don't compare yourself to other people. Figure out what your goal is — it doesn't have to be retirement by a certain age — then decide how you're going to do it, and ignore the noise.

CHAPTER 10

FAMILY AND FRUGALITY

When we first arrived in Iowa, I realized I hadn't prepared myself for this moment: waking up in my childhood bedroom in my parents' house in the tiny town where I grew up, next to my wife and baby, having just quit my job and given up my beach-town lifestyle.

If this was FIRE, it did not feel nearly as glamorous as I had imagined.

Bellevue, Iowa, is a beautiful little "Pleasantville" on the Mississippi River with limestone bluffs, rolling hills, and corn-fields for miles. Of the 2,100 people who live in Bellevue, I'm probably related in some way to at least 250 of them. That's 10 percent of the population! My parents were both born in Bel-levue, but my dad's job in the navy took us to San Diego (where I was born), Hawaii, Puerto Rico, the East Coast, and more. Our family returned to Iowa when I was entering my fresh-man year of high school. By then, I was a world traveler and adventure addict stuck in the body of a fast-talking thirteen-year-old. Bellevue couldn't have been more different from what I was used to. In high school, people often asked me if it was difficult as a kid moving from place to place. I never knew an alternate reality, so I would ask a similar question: "Was it difficult to grow up in the same place?" Personally, I loved the change, the exciting locations, and the chance to start over every couple of years, collecting friends and memories along the way. Now, returning as an adult to live and stay in Bellevue was the most significant culture shock I'd ever experienced.

Because of my upbringing, my relationship with Bellevue

has always been conflicted. I love to visit, love spending time with family, love to spend a week relaxing in my childhood home (which now includes watching my parents play with Jovie), and love feeling that there is somewhere in the world I belong. But true to my navy brat roots, I am a wanderer at heart. A couple of weeks in Iowa leaves me restless and stir-crazy, desperate for a bold adventure or a taste of big-city life.

So it was a bit ironic that my biggest and boldest adventure yet involved returning home, at least for a while. I hoped that my family would be accepting — excited even? — about Taylor's and my radical shift in perspective and our newfound simplistic lifestyle. After our trips to Ecuador and Dallas, we felt more comfortable discussing FIRE. I thought maybe I could interest them in the principles of FIRE: less consuming, more saving, more meaningful life decisions. In one of my grandiose moments, I imagined becoming a modern-day explorer, bringing the gift of FIRE to people otherwise stuck in lives of nine-to-five drudgery. Little did I know how backward I had it.

■ ■ ■ ■

One day in late October, Taylor and I invited my cousin Jared and my buddy Eric over to play cards and catch up. Eventually, the conversation turned to what Taylor and I were doing in Iowa. I started by explaining why we'd left Coronado: how we were pursuing the idea of living more frugally as a way of maximizing our happiness, since people typically spend most of their money on expensive items and experiences but get most of their joy from simple, free things like spending time together. With FIRE, I explained, you create a high savings rate and invest your money so that you can spend your time doing what you love.

At this point, I paused. Was I saying too much? I didn't want to sound judgmental or possibly offend these guys, the way these conversations had gone in Seattle.

Jared looked at me, confused. "I mean, isn't that how most people live?"

"Yeah," I said, nodding. "I think most people overspend and undersave."

"No," he said. "I mean, don't most people spend a lot less than they make and save the extra?"

I was dumbstruck. Here I thought I was going to blow Jared's and Eric's minds, and instead they looked at me like I had just explained that the sky is blue.

Jared already lived a frugal lifestyle, which seemed normal to him. He drove a fully paid-off car, he lived in a home that he'd helped build to save on costs, and he saved plenty of his income. He didn't want to stop working; he loved his job. He didn't have any grand plan. Living this way just made sense. Eric agreed — he always saved a portion of every dollar he earned. Why take out a big loan for a fancy car when it didn't get you anywhere faster than a regular car? As they both pointed out, this attitude and lifestyle are natural in a place like Bellevue, where almost every expense (housing, gas, health care, food, and so on) is cheaper than in a larger city.

I can only imagine what they said to each other on their drive home. Granted, there's more to FIRE than frugality, but they must have laughed their asses off at their genius friend Scotty who thought he had discovered the secret to life, something they had known all along.

Lying in bed that night, I came to a profound realization: I originally left home in order to find my way, but I had become lost. When I left Iowa after college, I wanted to see everything, experience everything, say yes to every invitation and opportunity that came my way. Ten years later, after countless cities and a whole lot of wasted money, I had returned trying to learn what my family back home had always known: Frugality is a type of freedom. This is my legacy; I come from a family of simplicity and contentment. But I had forgotten this, or perhaps I was never aware of it in the first place.

This unexpected realization was more than a little embarrassing, but it was also comforting. Maybe the universe has a plan after all. In my humble opinion, there is a reason folks in the Midwest have a reputation for friendliness (obviously, many other regions do too). You won't find many people filling their homes with expensive toys or buying cars they can't afford. Rather, they tend to value the most important things in life: connection, family, and friends. I couldn't be prouder to call myself a Hawkeye. I now recognize that in many ways the values and lifestyles of farm communities and towns like Bellevue reflect the utilitarian, simple values and sensible frugality of FIRE.

Not long after this, in early November, I went fishing with my cousin Chucky on his new boat, something both he and I had been looking forward to ever since I told him I was coming for an extended stay in Iowa. Growing up, Chucky was one of my closest friends — we were born two months apart — and our friendship had only gotten stronger as we got older.

After high school, Chucky and I took different paths: I headed off to a four-year college to get a liberal arts degree, and Chucky went to a two-year trade school to become an electrician. At the time, I considered it a given that I would be more successful, since I was getting a fancier degree. Only now did I fully appreciate how naïve that assumption was: Chucky started earning money and building his career while I was still racking up student debt for two more years. A decade later, he clearly had a higher net worth than me. But, in my newly formed opinion, he still worked too many hours away from his family and had started buying expensive toys just as I had. I felt like Chucky, with his inquisitive nature, would find the FIRE framework more than intriguing. Plus, I knew for a fact that he would much rather go fishing than to work most days.

So, early one morning I met Chucky at Lock and Dam 12 on the Mississippi River. His new boat was beautiful — equipped with comfortable elevated seats, rod holders, and a brand-new GPS-enabled trolling motor that would automatically keep us in whichever spot was producing the most bites (if we could find that spot!). We'd barely had time to tie the knots on our fishing lines when he asked me what the hell I was doing. He knew that I had quit my job and was moving home for a few months, but he didn't know any of the details — or, most importantly, about FIRE. Somewhat anxiously, since I didn't want to make things awkward between us (the way it had been with too many of these encounters), I explained the basics — about FIRE, the documentary, our search for a new hometown, and our long-term plan to reach financial freedom in about a decade and be able to stop working.

Chucky was certainly open to the idea, but he was confused. He felt he already lived the FIRE formula. He worked hard, made good money as an electrician, and invested a healthy portion of his earnings with a local money manager. He wasn't sure exactly how much he was saving, but it was a lot. So, he asked me, if he was already taking the steps necessary, was it actually possible that he wouldn't have to work until he was sixty-five?

It was, I told him. In fact, he was closer to FIRE than I was! I said it would be crazy to keep working until sixty-five if he didn't have to.

"I don't spend a lot," Chucky said. "Besides, my truck is paid off, and my house will be paid off in ten years. I'm barely in debt." But I had a hard time explaining how this translated into being able to retire early, and Chucky grew defensive when I said he had to change his spending and level of debt to achieve FIRE. I realized (too late) that his brand-new $19,000 fishing boat may not have been the best location for this conversation.

I decided to back off. In the past, I had become too dogmatic about FIRE too quickly. The last thing I wanted was for

Chucky to think I was judging him — and how could I, when Taylor and I had succumbed to lifestyle creep in the worst way?

That night, I sent him more information on low-cost index funds and some links to good blogs and podcasts, and I left it at that.

■ ■ ■ ■

The rest of November flew by in a blur of playing with Jovie, writing, producing the documentary, and playing cards around the kitchen table with family and friends. I enjoyed the kind of quality time with my family that I'd rarely experienced during our normal, short vacations to see them. On one particular Friday, I spent the better part of the day outside with my dad replacing a large section of the fence that borders the back of my parents' property. Wherever possible, we also cut limbs overhanging the fence line to prevent them from falling and creating more repairs in the future. The operation involved strategic tree trimming, cutting larger branches into logs, and throwing the leftovers into piles for later burning. It was a cold, brisk day — the kind of weather that I loved as a kid. My dad and I had a great time, working hard, talking, and even daydreaming about ways we could one day join forces to buy rental properties and fix them up together (I think I liked that idea better than he did). The sweat, the cold, the sore feet, my shoulders burning from holding a saw over my head for ten minutes straight while standing in the bucket of a tractor raised up fifteen feet in the air: OSHA may not have approved, but Mr. Money Mustache certainly would have.

When we went back inside, Jovie was playing on her grandmother's lap, and Taylor was working on the couch. I went and sat next to my mom, and we talked about how amazing it had been for her and my dad to spend so much time with Jovie. In the past when Taylor and I had come to Iowa, it was for a

FAMILY AND FRUGALITY

week at a time and we both would be decompressing from work while trying to cram as much into our vacation as we could. This meant I didn't get to spend the quiet, everyday moments with my family like I would have wanted. My parents, especially my mom, had supported me and Taylor so much with this project — from helping us move to watching Jovie while we filmed for the documentary to providing emotional support during my many moments of doubt. It was amazing to think that if I had never heard that Tim Ferriss podcast episode, I wouldn't be there right then in Iowa watching my mom play with Jovie.

For me, it was a blissful moment, one of many I experienced early in our journey, that epitomized our goals and the FIRE philosophy. We were traveling outside our comfort zone in search of a happier existence. At times, it was hard — hopping from home to home, living with our parents, having all our stuff in storage, not knowing where we were going to land — but the discomfort served a purpose that, on particular days like this, made it all worth it. Being with my family all together in one place, working outdoors with my dad, spending time with my mom — these simple pleasures felt like a sign that we were on the right track.

■ ■ ■ ■

By early December, our time in Iowa was almost over. We planned to return to Seattle a week before Christmas to spend the holidays with Taylor's family, and then after New Year's we would start our three-month-long test drive of Bend. It had been a successful trip, and even though Taylor and I both felt like we had become much closer to my family, we were excited to get started on our hunt for our new home.

A few days later, my mom asked what gifts Taylor and I wanted for Christmas, and all that good feeling vanished.

Taylor and I exchanged wide-eyed looks over the table. We hadn't planned for Christmas gifts in our budget, and as my mom discussed her plans, this simple expectation, this annual ritual of appreciation and love, caused us to completely fall apart.

My mom explained what she was getting for some of our relatives, and she reminded us of several upcoming holiday parties, for which we should bring some simple gifts for the party hosts. But the only "gift fund" Taylor and I had to pull from was our $150 monthly "shopping" budget, and we'd already blown much of that on wine, chocolate, paper towels, laundry detergent, and other odds and ends. Never mind what Taylor and I wanted for Christmas. How were we going to afford gifts for our parents, Jovie, Taylor's sister and brother-in-law, our nieces, her grandmother, and all our friends?

In the past, Taylor and I had regularly spent over $1,500 on Christmas gifts, and we put a lot of thought into those gifts, so they expressed how much each person meant to us. We thought of ourselves as generous people, and still do. Yet somehow, in all our budget plans and our eagerness to reach FIRE, we'd completely forgotten about Christmas, and we hadn't set aside any money to be generous with.

I knew we couldn't keep spending $1,500, but I couldn't imagine having Christmas without getting *anything* for our families. Not only would that be rude and ungrateful to the people who were generously hosting us, but it would be like thumbing our noses at a tradition and custom we had enjoyed our entire lives. Christmas gifts weren't some bad spending habit we had developed as we got older. This was a part of our childhoods, deeply rooted in our memories, and part of family bonding.

Alone in our bedroom, Taylor and I strategized how to stretch the $93.22 left in our "shopping" fund into gifts for everyone. It was hopeless, and soon the discussion shifted to the amount of stress and energy our frugality was costing us, which was starting to overshadow everything else. Just a week earlier, we were feeling cooped up in my parents' house; for four straight days, we'd eaten at home with my parents and barely left the house other than for an occasional walk. We'd vowed to break our habit of eating out, but that plan had gotten old fast, and we had really wanted to go out for dinner. So we said, "Screw it," gave in to our desire, and ate at a restaurant with nice reviews and a four-star rating on Yelp. Lo and behold, the food was subpar compared to my mother's cooking, and we ended the night filled with buyer's remorse. We had let our old selves take over, and it hadn't even been worth it!

Despite how hard frugality was to live day after day, I still didn't want to give up. I looked at our budget for places to cut back and suggested maybe we stop drinking beer and wine, which we both were enjoying a bit more frequently during all this chaos.

"When I agreed to leave San Diego, I told you I wasn't giving up wine and chocolate," Taylor said. "I've given up my home and my car. I've left my friends. I'm living with my in-laws. This is where I draw the line."

She was right, and hearing her say it out loud reminded me of how much we'd already given up. In the space of a couple of months, we had flipped our life (and expenses) inside out. And it still wasn't enough. If we were having trouble sticking to our $4,200-a-month budget now, how hard would it be once we added the cost of rent or a mortgage? How much more would we have to give up? And even if we could do it now, what about five years from now? What about when we reached financial independence? Is this what our "retirement" was going to look like, a life without restaurant dinners, Christmas gift-giving, or trips to foreign countries?

I hadn't fully admitted it to myself, but the truth was that I had become disenchanted, overwhelmed, and frustrated with the FIRE lifestyle. The rush of excitement as we'd made these big decisions had worn off, and we were left with this: the same work life as before but with fewer luxuries and conveniences. The thrill of committing ourselves to a life of low expenses was gone.

In fact, I'd reached the moment I'd always wondered about when other people described how they had achieved financial independence through FIRE. Did they ever get depressed always picking the frugal option? Didn't they ever just want to throw budgets to the wind and live a little?

I had other concerns about FIRE. A few months before, I had read an article called "Financially Independent Retired Early: Flaws with the Philosophy?" One flaw that the article described was the magnitude of potential lost income. The FIRE community focuses intently on the incredible earning power of those ten to fifteen years of wealth accumulation that lead up to the early retirement date. However, as this article pointed out, if you actually retire early, you stop saving, and you lose the compounding of your investments for the next twenty to thirty years (up to the typical retirement age), which are typically the highest earning years in a career. Retiring early also diminishes someone's contribution to Social Security, which lowers their Social Security benefits in later years. And is it possible that the FIRE lifestyle (frugality combined with jobless parents) sets a bad example for children?

As we talked, Taylor and I quickly fell down a dark rabbit hole of fear and doubt. What if one of us had a medical emergency? What if our families needed help financially and we couldn't give it to them? How would we save for Jovie's college fund if we weren't working? Finally, we both agreed that we needed to sleep on our worries and talk them over in the morning. Somehow, in order to keep going, we had to shake off our anxiety, recapture some of our initial excitement about FIRE, and remember why we were doing all this in the first place.

SAVE FOR COLLEGE OR SAVE FOR FIRE?

FIRE families sometimes feel they have to choose: Should they save to retire early or to pay for their children's college? What is the better attitude to take with kids — "Let them fend for themselves" or "Set 'em up for life"? This is something Taylor and I have spoken about a lot, and while we have no concrete answer, our current plan is to get Jovie's compound interest calculator started early by pushing her to contribute to a Roth IRA as soon as she starts working. We also plan on talking to Jovie about all the FIRE-approved methods for hacking college, like attending a community college, focusing on scholarships, living at home, or working during the summer to cover her tuition. Taylor and I have decided not to contribute to a 529 plan (or a college savings account) because we think having a considerable amount of money tied up in a fund that can only be used for a specific purpose doesn't provide enough flexibility for us or for Jovie. Part of financial independence is being able to use your money as you choose.

The next morning, I was feeling just as stressed and doubtful. I wanted to have a quiet breakfast alone with Taylor and Jovie, but of course my parents were there, so we couldn't. I resented their presence, and I felt worse for feeling this way: My parents were putting us up, cleaning up after us, providing free daycare, and feeding us, and I knew full well how lucky we were. And I'm sure it wasn't roses for them, either. I appreciated all that my parents were doing for us, but I missed our former lives in San Diego. I missed our friends. For a fleeting moment, I even missed the comfort of my old job.

Had I screwed up? Taylor and I had made an agreement before starting our journey: At any moment, we could pull the rip cord and go back to Coronado. Was it time? That sounded so wonderful. December in Iowa is damn cold, and it would be a breezy 65 degrees back in California. Taylor looked at me from across the kitchen table, and I knew she was thinking the same thing.

I spent the morning reading negative articles about FIRE on the internet and tweaking our budget so we could afford Christmas gifts. When that got old, I decided mending fences would be a nice escape. I put on some work clothes and braved the cold to help my dad on his fence project. For a while we worked in silence, cutting the limbs faster and more efficiently than before. Then he mentioned that Taylor and I seemed stressed and asked if everything was okay. I filled him in on some of our worries about frugal living and the sacrifices we were making.

"Am I condemning my family to a life of frugality when we could be living by the beach?" I asked. My dad laughed and said, "Kiddo, take a look around." He pointed out that he and my mom had always lived frugally even when they could afford more. My father grew up in a no-frills household, with food on the table and a roof over his head but not much else, so he understands what it feels like to go without. "We didn't have much when we were your age. We lived on little and worked long hours just like you. We get it."

I shared all my doubts: that we were rushing, impulsively jumping into the FIRE lifestyle with both feet. And what was I thinking trying to film a documentary about a lifestyle choice I was still in the process of understanding? After all, I'd only heard about this idea a few months before, and I'd made a series of major life decisions because of it.

"Well, you've always been impulsive," he said. "You get an idea, and you run with it. Ready, fire, aim." He was right. My adult life was filled with passion projects marked by meteoric spikes of enthusiasm and often followed by slowly waning interest. Then, it was on to the next one.

"But what if this is a really bad idea? What if it doesn't work?"

My dad paused, and in a fatherly tone he told me bluntly that some of the projects and endeavors I had pursued over the years had made little sense to him. But somehow I had proved him wrong over and over again. And this time, he thought FIRE was a winner. "Scott, this project is different. You are onto something with this FIRE thing and with this documentary. We are really surprised and proud of you both. We never saw you leaving Coronado. Stick with it."

Further, he said my mom had read the book I'd given them, *The Simple Path to Wealth* by JL Collins, done some additional research, and decided to switch all their retirement savings to Vanguard and start investing in index funds. If this was a bad idea, he said, well, then he was fooled right along with me.

A few hours later, I got a text from Chucky: He'd signed up for a budgeting tool and added, "I hate seeing how much I spend on dumb shit!! And I'll admit, it's pretty awesome." So, our fishing trip had been a success after all. One of my favorite people in the world had caught the FIRE bug. Seeing that was a relief after all the worry and doubt I had been feeling.

■ ■ ■ ■

After this, my anxiety about FIRE calmed down, but I decided to call Brandon, a.k.a. the Mad Fientist, and ask him about my concerns: Was I overreacting? Were my concerns legitimate? Had he experienced the same doubts? If so, how had he dealt with them? Brandon listened patiently and acknowledged that he'd had similar struggles early in his journey. He had seen how pursuing frugality to extremes can lead to depression and isolation from other people. He said that he and I clearly shared one trait: impatience. He drove home the message that I needed to beware of obsessing over FIRE and frugality to the peril of my daily happiness. Pete from *Mr. Money Mustache* also makes this point in a blog post titled "Happiness Is the Only Logical Pursuit." In it, Pete argues that we should focus not on money but on understanding what makes us truly happy, and then make choices that improve our long-term happiness.

Next, I asked Brandon about a more practical financial concern: What if the market doesn't perform as well as predicted? In a way, we were gambling our entire lifestyle on a set of financial assumptions that, if they didn't hold, might render our sacrifices meaningless. This is a topic of very real debate and concern in the FIRE community, and Brandon walked me through the numbers (for a summary of this, see "What Actually Happens If the Stock Market Crashes," page 41). The upshot is that "financial independence" is entirely self-defined. How much you need to save, and for how long, depends on how much you spend, the rate of inflation, the actual market returns you achieve, and hundreds of other factors. The specific numbers aside, Brandon emphasized that patience and flexibility are vital ingredients in a sound FIRE plan. Focusing on reaching financial independence by a predetermined date and obsessing about market returns and every expenditure can be detrimental. If you follow the core FIRE principles — spend less than you earn, and save at a high rate — you will reach early retirement, so does it really matter if that's in eight, ten, or twelve years? Or if it takes even longer because markets dip for an extended period? "It's going to be what it's going to be," he said, and he reminded me that most people, after reaching FIRE, continue to work and generate income because they are pursuing their passions. In reality, a person's pre-FIRE and post-FIRE lives can end up blending together seamlessly. The specific date you reach financial independence is either a blurry moving target or simply a checkmark on a calendar. "Set a course and go live your life," Brandon advised.

"But what about the lost-wages flaw?" I asked. Was retiring

even a worthwhile goal if it meant losing earnings of $100,000 a year for twenty years, which equated to forgoing nearly $7 million? Brandon laughed.

"Scott," he said, "FIRE is about figuring out what you need to live a happy life. What do you need $7 million for? To buy a boat club membership and a BMW?"

Ouch. But he was right. Back at the start, when Taylor and I had listed all the things that make us happy, we named experiences and connection with loved ones, not luxuries or conveniences. Not $7 million.

Brandon reiterated, "It's not about the money. The money is a vehicle to optimizing your life experience. Now go and study that."

■ ■ ■ ■

Since then, I've learned that Taylor's and my experiences in Iowa were not only perfectly normal but something of a rite of passage for people pursuing FIRE. We got too extreme too fast. We were excited about FIRE and tried to cut out every possible expense instead of thinking about what would be sustainable for the long haul. When the honeymoon phase ended, we found ourselves committed to a life where we were barely spending any money and having to face the fact that extreme frugality just *isn't that much fun*.

And of course, everyone's idea of extreme frugality is different. For some people, that's spending $10,000 a year; for others, it's spending $100,000 a year. For us, it was the point where we started caring more about saving money than we did about enjoying life, ourselves, and time with other people. The tricky part is that it's easy to use personal enjoyment as a rationalization for spending $200 on sushi dinners with friends. That isn't the answer. But neither is not buying Christmas presents and always drinking the cheapest possible wine. Taylor and I had to find a middle ground between deprivation and indulgence.

One of my mentors on this topic is J. D. Roth, the creator of the blog *Get Rich Slowly*. J. D. started one of the first personal finance blogs in order to hold himself accountable: He wanted to pay off his debt and get his spending under control. It worked: A year later J. D. became debt-free for the first time in his life. Then his blog grew, becoming one of the most popular personal finance blogs, and he eventually sold it for enough money that he could become financially independent. In the FIRE community, J. D. focuses on the emotions and psychology behind FIRE (versus just the cold, hard numbers). He has spent a lot of time thinking about the *why* of financial independence.

Recently, J. D. helped me create a personal mission statement. This exercise is powerful for anyone, regardless of financial situation, but it's especially powerful for someone pursuing FIRE, who may be putting all their eggs in the "when I'm retired, I'll be happy" basket. The exercise involves answering three questions:

- What are your most important life goals?
- What would you do if you only had six months to live?
- How do you want to spend the next five years?

Here's how I answered those questions:

- My family is everything to me, so my most important life goal is being available to them as much as I can. Sometimes my head can be lost in the future, so my life goal is also being present and in-the-moment when I am spending time with my family.
- If I had six months to live, I would spend as much time as I could with my family (see above) and try to spend time reflecting on my life.
- I'm a dreamer, so I love thinking about the future! I want to spend the next five years satisfying my

entrepreneurial drive while helping as many people as possible (including myself and my family!)
reach FI.

Finally, you combine all your answers into a single mission
statement. Here's the one I ultimately came up with:

I will be present for those who love me and rely on me.
I will live a rich, happy, and fulfilling life, and I will
empower others to do the same.

People like Brandon and J. D. have helped me see that FIRE
is not about saving every last penny and trying to reach retirement as soon as humanly possible. It's about building a lifestyle
that aligns with your larger life purpose, *even while you are still
working.* "Retirement" isn't the answer to every problem. With
FIRE, it's just a natural outcome of aligning your values with
your choices.

So what happened that Christmas? By the time we left
Iowa to head back to Seattle for the holidays, we had solved the
gift problem: Jovie was so young, we could have wrapped up
a can of soup, and she would have been elated. So we wrapped
some secondhand books, and she loved them. We bought new
presents for our nieces, as we didn't want to inflict our new
lifestyle on their memories and traditions. We decided to forgo
presents for friends, which was easy while we were on the road.
No one noticed. Finally, we got our family to agree to a long-
term solution: Instead of focusing on gifts, we would all focus
on low-cost experiences and time spent together. We created an
annual Secret Santa drawing so that we will each get to have a
fun experience with another family member. This way, we will
generate fun and new memories with our loved ones that we
will cherish forever. That is worth every penny. Frugal? Not
completely. But intentional? Absolutely.

Looking ahead, gift-giving occasions are something that
Taylor and I are still figuring out. How do we honor the spirit

of the occasion while protecting our financial goals? How do we show people how much they matter to us without using money and gifts? Further, what works for one occasion, or for one year or even five years, won't necessarily always work. As Jovie gets older, she will have different expectations around gifts, our lifestyle will change, and our finances will change. Currently, though, we are planning on putting aside $50 a month toward a gift fund.

The real lesson we learned that particular Christmas was the need to be flexible. We were reminded that any frugality that causes harm and stress to our lives does not qualify as a principle of FIRE.

CHAPTER 11

DREAM HOUSE OR DREAM LIFE?

Bend was our dream town.

After only a few weeks of living there, we realized we had fallen completely in love with it and didn't need to consider any alternatives.

Bend is bikeable, outdoorsy, and affordable enough for our FIRE budget. It offers nearly three hundred days of sunshine a year and a world-class microbrew scene. While I was still living in San Diego, I read a *Washington Post* article about Bend, and I found it hard to believe the hype. The article read:

> The city — the largest in Central Oregon — boasts 71 parks and 48 miles of recreational trails. Less than an hour outside town, you'll find 26 golf courses, whitewater rafting and fly-fishing in the Deschutes River, more than 1,000 climbing routes and 3,600 skiable acres at Mount Bachelor.... You can paddleboard on one of the 40 lakes in the region, hike and camp in the Three Sisters Wilderness, or summit Pilot Butte, a 479-foot-tall cinder cone in the center of town. Or just find something that floats — an inner tube, an inflatable mattress — and drift on a mellow stretch of Deschutes from Bend Park to the center of town; a $5 shuttle gets you back to your car.... And *Dog Fancy* magazine called Bend the most dog-friendly city in the country. It's hard to say what the city *doesn't* do perfectly.

As we got to know Bend, I had to admit that the glowing reviews seemed accurate. And the article hadn't even mentioned the great schools!

Over those first few weeks, we explored Bend thoroughly. We visited parks and nearby towns; we joined the US Forest Service for a free guided snowshoeing hike in the beautiful Deschutes National Forest. We fell in love with the lack of traffic, the proximity to wilderness, and Bend's overall laid-back nature. I never wasted time driving around looking for a parking spot, and during a single grocery store trip, I was asked for cooking advice and people made eye contact, smiled, and held the door for me as I walked out with an armful of groceries. Bend combined the excitement and amenities of a big city with the sense of community of a small town.

Plus, after months of wandering from place to place, crashing on couches or squeezing into guest bedrooms, Taylor and I were grateful to be settled in one spot and to have an entire house all to ourselves. Originally we had planned on renting in Bend for a year or so and getting the lay of the land, but we scrapped those plans and decided to start our house hunt after just a few weeks. Even though we were scheduled to be house-sitting in Hawaii from April to June, we were hoping to find a house beforehand so we could lock in a low interest rate. Besides, we wanted to take our time finding a new home in Bend, and we didn't want to waste a year's worth of rent that could be building equity in a house.

■ ■ ■ ■

Before we bought a house, we had to buy a car — specifically, a car that cost around $5,000. I wanted to follow Brandon's advice as closely as possible: Spend $5,000, and avoid a gas-guzzler. There was just one small problem: winter. As we were experiencing, this mountainous area gets serious snowstorms, and the temps can stay in the teens for a week at a time. Roads can be icy and steep. I wanted a gas-sipping car, but after slipping and sliding in our front-wheel-drive Mazda 3, I knew a four-wheel- or all-wheel-drive (AWD) vehicle was in our future. I dove into Craigslist, and scoured Bend, but I quickly learned that finding a car with AWD for $5,000 was asking a lot. Feeling frustrated, I increased our budget a tad to see what popped up.

Bingo. I found a Toyota 4Runner, my ideal choice, in immaculate condition with only 100,000 miles and one owner for $12,500. Cheap for a 4Runner in that condition! The next day with my dad, who was visiting us in Bend, I checked out the car. My dad thought it was the perfect vehicle for us, one that would probably run another 100,000 miles with no issues. But my FIRE senses were uncertain. The 4Runner only got 16 miles per gallon (mpg), and it cost two and a half times my prescribed budget.

Just before we saw the 4Runner, I also came across a 2006 AWD Honda CRV with 179,000 miles for $7,500. Interesting. I booked a test drive of the CRV: It was very roomy inside, the engine purred, it got 25 mpg, and the maintenance records were immaculate. Plus, it had a brand-new set of snow tires! Despite the high mileage, the car had been regularly serviced and had only one owner, so I figured the odds were good the Honda engine would continue to purr. Also, even if I only got a few good years out of the car, that would still be better financially than the depreciation I would experience with my Mazda. If it went longer, that would be icing on the cake. I was also resolved to bike as much as possible, so this would give me added incentive: The fewer miles I racked up on the car, the longer the car might last, the less we would spend on gas, and the less we would pollute the earth.

After evaluating the market, I decided to offer $6,500 for

the CRV. They accepted, and boom, we drove away in our new (FIRE-approved) car. It wasn't $5,000, but it was close enough.

Parking the CRV in our driveway that night, I realized this was the first time in my adult life that I had paid cash for a vehicle and owned it outright. As a thirty-four-year-old, I wasn't sure whether to be happy or to cry myself to sleep. Either way, it was another win for the FIRE lifestyle. Now that we had a frugal used car, I listed my Mazda lease on a transfer site and got ready to start house shopping.

■ ■ ■ ■

The only problem with our new dream city was that it seemed like it was everybody else's dream city, too. Bend housing prices had risen since our time in Ecuador — when we had budgeted $1,500 for renting a house and $400,000 for buying a house — let alone since we'd first researched Bend while still living in San Diego. Based on online research, our budget had seemed realistic, and Taylor and I had envisioned our Bend home with three bedrooms, floor-to-ceiling windows, a big backyard with room to build a work studio, and all within walking or biking distance of a brewery or two. After all, I had promised Taylor that leaving San Diego would allow us to find a place with the same quality of life at a cheaper price. Owning a beautiful home in a walkable neighborhood was a key aspect of what we thought would bring us happiness.

Now we weren't feeling as optimistic. As we came to understand the geography, neighborhoods, and school districts, we realized most of the houses we had seen online were prohibitively far from the city center or in really bad condition. Good houses in the neighborhoods we wanted were being snatched up quickly with multiple cash offers and often with bids over the asking price. In the neighborhoods we could afford, houses were often too small for us (under a thousand square feet), or we'd be forced to drive to get anywhere.

"I thought if we came to Bend, we wouldn't have to compromise," Taylor said when I tried to convince us both that we didn't actually *need* three bedrooms. "The move was the compromise." She was right. We had compromised by leaving the place we loved. We hadn't planned on having to compromise on the house we bought.

Then we found our dream house. It was set back in the hills on a quarter-acre lot within walking distance of a coffee shop, a neighborhood market, and a couple of restaurants. It had a big deck overlooking a giant yard. The midcentury modern design offered a wall of windows in the living room with a view of big, beautiful pines. As soon as Taylor stepped into the living room and saw that view, she was sold.

"This is our house," she whispered to me while we toured the backyard, complete with a work studio and a chicken coop. I felt the same way — this house literally *felt* like our house. Even if we had built a house from scratch, I'm not sure that it would have felt as made for us as this house did.

The only issue was that it was *slightly* over our budget — the asking price was $480,000, not the $400,000 we preferred. Maybe all the money saved on eggs would offset the cost?

As we left, we rationalized that in San Diego we'd been prepared to spend well over $500,000 for a barely habitable townhouse an hour from Coronado. To get a dream home in a perfect Bend location, we'd spend $20,000 less. We brainstormed ways to cut back on other expenses to make it possible to afford this house.

"Maybe we'll just extend our FI date," I said. "If we were willing to work just a few years longer, we could make this house work." She looked hesitant. Every year we kept working was another year of getting older.

"What if I tried to land a couple of big commissions this

year?" Taylor suggested. Part of her income was based on commission, and she always had the opportunity to take on more clients. "I could work a few more hours a week for the rest of the year, and we could bridge the gap that way."

A nagging voice inside my head piped up, saying, *Maybe this isn't such a good idea.* After all, a main philosophy of FIRE is that you always buy or rent less house than you can afford. When Taylor and I left California, one main goal was to stop paying so much in housing costs and start saving that money.

Our realtor had told us that this house would most likely go quickly; if we wanted to put in an offer, we should do it as soon as possible. When Taylor and I got home, we decided to walk around the neighborhood and try to come to a decision. The sun was setting as we put Jovie in her stroller and went out. The forecast predicted snow that night, but for now the sky was clear and still. After a while, Taylor took my hand and said, "I honestly never thought I could be happy living somewhere that wasn't Coronado, but I was wrong."

I nodded. I told her that Bend felt like the kind of town we'd been looking for all along; we just hadn't known it. We daydreamed about raising Jovie in a town this quiet and safe, about the outdoor adventures we would have with her, especially if we weren't working. The fact that Taylor felt this way was intoxicating, as my fear of failing her continued to melt away.

"Let's do it," I said. "Let's buy this house."

We stopped on the sidewalk while I called the realtor and told her that we wanted to make an offer. That night, we opened a bottle of wine and drank to our future: a new life in a new home in a new city.

■ ■ ■ ■

The next day the realtor called to say the house had multiple offers, and if we were serious, we needed to raise ours.

"We're already over our budget," I told her. "How much higher do we need to go?"

She said, to stay in the running, we should offer over $500,000. We had come full circle, back to our original California budget. This was not why we'd left. This wasn't FIRE.

But I thought: *This isn't just any house — this is our house! The house we have always dreamed of buying, our forever home.* Besides, if Bend was this popular now, how much would our house be worth in five or ten years? We decided to raise our offer by $25,000, which made it $505,000.

An hour after putting in the higher offer, I knew we had made a mistake. In the course of one week, we had raised our house budget by over $100,000. The issue was more than the house or the cost; it was how we were slipping back into our old mindset around money. We had changed our surroundings, changed our cars, and even changed our spending, but we were still rationalizing big purchases in the same way. We still felt we deserved the "ultimate" thing and we shouldn't have to compromise to get what we wanted. But if we really wanted our time back, buying a $500,000 house was more of a setback than an opportunity.

As Taylor and I were walking back from a local park with Jovie, I couldn't hold back this lingering doubt any longer. I told Taylor I didn't feel comfortable paying half a million dollars for a house, especially if we were serious about FIRE. I brought up the quality-of-life lists we'd written in California. Neither mentioned a beautiful house with giant windows. None of the things that brought us happiness required vaulted ceilings or a brand-new kitchen. If we weren't careful, our dream house might actually hold us back from our real dreams.

"I'm not sure that I'm going to be happy with the kind of house we can afford in Bend," Taylor said.

Maybe, she suggested, we needed to keep looking at other, more-affordable cities. After all, we left San Diego to escape its high cost of living, and here we were having the same conversations, just in a new city.

I wasn't ready to give up on Bend, even though I agreed with her logic: If our goal was to get our time back, wouldn't it make sense to move to the cheapest possible place and buy the cheapest possible house? I remembered Brandon's warning about being too extreme. What was the right balance for us between everyday satisfaction and our FIRE plans? How could we maximize our savings without turning it into deprivation? What was the difference between unneeded luxuries and purchases that brought true happiness?

Then I remembered an interview with financial expert Michael Kitces on a *Mad Fientist* podcast. In the moment I only recalled the gist of what he'd said, but here is the full passage from the episode:

> I've spent most of my life living in houses that are, at worst, 20 percent of my income. Most of the time, I've lived in housing that's less than 10 percent of my income. And when you spend less than 10 percent of your income on housing, all that stuff about whether you should save money buying a five-dollar Starbucks coffee or not — I don't give a crap. I just go buy the coffee. You know what? If I feel like buying it, I just stop and buy it. I don't care. When you get the big stuff right, and when you manage the recurring stuff, it's actually amazing how not much the one-off stuff even adds up to at that point.

Taylor and I both knew that these larger purchase decisions are the real make-or-break when it comes to FIRE. Stressing about whether to splurge on an expensive brand-name cold brew is one thing; stressing about a house payment is a whole other level. But as Kitces says, if you eliminate the big stresses, the little ones often go away, too.

This house wasn't the answer. I called the realtor and told her we wanted to withdraw our offer. Taylor and I agreed that, during our trip to Hawaii, we needed to consider other cities. Maybe Bend was too good to be true after all.

How a Fire Pushed Our Family to Reevaluate It All

By the Numbers

Pre-FI career: Dietitian
Current age: 36
Projected age at FI: 46
Current annual spending: $50,000

What FIRE Means to Me

One night in October, my husband, Jesse, and I found ourselves packing our belongings in the middle of the night and fleeing from a raging wildfire less than a mile from our house. The wildfire created a tangible sense of impermanence and helped us let go of the future we had imagined and open ourselves to the future that could be. We decided that if we let go of the house, let go of the high-cost-of-living area, let go of our stable jobs, and challenged the conventional paradigm of "success," we could open ourselves up to discover a life with more freedom, adventure, and fulfillment.

My Path to FIRE

Before we found FIRE, we lived in Sonoma County in California with our two kids. Although together we made over $100,000 per year, we weren't saving money. We had drawn a typical future for ourselves in our head: a mortgage, two kids, the cat, the dog, the daily grind of working hard in a high-cost-of-living area. We started listening to podcasts about minimalism and financial independence with the hope of teaching ourselves how to live a life closer to our values. Our eyes opened. It felt like we were coming out of a deep, mindless consumer slumber.

It was right around this time that we woke up one night to the smell of smoke and the rumble of 80-mile-per-hour winds. After running outside and feeling the hot wind and seeing nothing but a wall of smoke in the sky, instincts kicked in and we decided to get out. I took a few minutes to throw some sentimental items and essentials into a suitcase. As I did that, I looked at each of my things through a different lens: Was it worth throwing in the suitcase or not? In ten minutes, we were out of our house. We didn't know if we would be coming back to a house or a pile of ashes. The wildfire swept through our town, taking down over five thousand homes. It was the most devastating wildfire in California history, and it came within a mile of our house. Many of our friends lost everything that night. Some lost lives. In the coming weeks, as we returned to our house, we realized that the time to make a change was now because clearly tomorrow was not guaranteed.

So we got rid of two-thirds of our stuff, quit our jobs, sold our house, left our hometown, said goodbye to family and friends, and set off with our two young children (then ages seven and one) across the country to find our new home. Over four months, we drove more than eleven thousand miles, traversed twenty-six states, visited five graduate schools, and saw fourteen different friends and family members, all on a total budget of less than $140 per day. Traveling for that long with our children was hard — and essential to strengthening our bond as a family. I had job interviews along the way and found a wonderful job opportunity in Denver, which is where our trip ended.

In a Nutshell

✓ We made reasonable financial choices as young adults but had a fairly typical start to our journey.

- ✓ We paid $380,000 for our first house and sold it for $600,000 four years later, a price jump due in part to a natural disaster.
- ✓ We are closer to FI now that we've left California but still seven to eight years away.
- ✓ We consider ourselves just starting on the path and feel like we still have a lot to learn.

The Hardest Part

Realizing that part of our FI journey was going to be to sell a house we loved and leave our friends and family behind to find a lower-cost area with better job opportunities. We had pictured ourselves raising our kids and growing old in that house, so selling it was one of the hardest steps we faced. The excitement of our next move (and the profit we made on the house) bolstered us, but the loss and grief we felt were also very real.

The Best Part

Feeling like we have choices and autonomy in creating the life we want, based on our dreams and fulfillment, rather than relying on the empty promises of consumer culture.

My Advice to You

Embracing discomfort and taking risks can open up possibilities that can bring you closer to a future that you really want.

CHAPTER 12

FINDING OUR FIRE FRIENDS

"Are you sure we're going the right way?" Taylor asked nervously. We were thirty miles east of Seattle, and our route had turned from a freeway into a two-lane highway into a winding country road overshadowed by forests. We had no cell service.

It was late May 2018 and we were headed to Camp Mustache, the annual meeting of Mustachians, and I was worried that I had talked Taylor into coming to something that was not going to be her cup of tea.

For the past two months, we had been staying on Kauai, housesitting for some friends of Taylor's family. In an unforeseen twist of fate, our trip coincided with the island's heaviest rainfall in recorded history, which caused massive mudslides and flash flooding and closed many of the roads and beaches. Because of this, our idyllic time in paradise hadn't gone according to plan. We'd planned on saving money by enjoying the beach every day and entertaining ourselves with the natural wonders of Hawaii. Since the storms made that challenging, we'd spent the last few weeks cooped up in our friends' house, frustrated that our budget meant we couldn't distract ourselves by going to the movies or going out to eat like we normally would have. At one point we broke down and went to a nice restaurant for a $100 seafood dinner. It was delicious, so we didn't have buyer's remorse, just a bit of budgeter's remorse.

Since we were supposed to stay in Hawaii until June, we hadn't planned on going to Camp Mustache. And it seemed unlikely that we would have been able to get tickets (the sixty spots usually sell out in minutes). So when one of the attendees had a work trip come up and offered to sell us his two tickets, we felt like we couldn't turn down the opportunity. We were ready to leave Hawaii, and we needed a dose of inspiration to help us stick with our new frugal budget. We used some old credit card points to book a flight to Sea-Tac, left Jovie with Taylor's parents, and drove from Seattle to spend the weekend with a bunch of FIRE enthusiasts.

At last, my headlights caught a small wooden sign next to a gravel path, and pretty soon we were parking in front of a big lodge. We had arrived at camp.

WHAT *EXACTLY* IS A MUSTACHIAN?

Officially, a Mustachian is anyone who follows the writings of Pete Adeney, a.k.a. Mr. Money Mustache. In the FIRE community, the "Mustachian" label has come to represent a certain way of thinking. Following the guidelines laid out in Pete's writing, Mustachians are very frugal and aim to keep their expenses under $40,000 a year. They try to minimize consumption in every way — from cutting out consumer purchases to buying a more fuel-efficient car or giving up their car entirely to keeping their house cool in the winter to reduce utility usage. They make decisions in line with their values instead of what mainstream culture dictates. They take pride in DIY accomplishment, whether it's fixing their own cars, using credit card rewards to hack their travel costs, or installing solar panels. Perhaps one of the primary guidelines of Mustachianism is to be rational and thoughtful about life decisions — from home purchases to health to vacations to friendships — and always, always optimize for happiness.

When I first got our tickets for Camp Mustache, I was determined to bring the film crew along to do interviews. Its four days of workshops, group discussions, hiking, and hanging out with other Mustachians would be the perfect opportunity to interview and film a group of FIRE people being themselves. It took a fair amount of convincing, but eventually the event organizers agreed to let my five-person crew (including the director, Travis) join the retreat for a full day.

Camp Mustache would also be a chance for me and Taylor to (hopefully) make new friends. I knew we needed to build a community of people who were pursuing FIRE, for both moral and logistical support. Constantly feeling like we were swimming against the mainstream was hard, and we were always relieved to hang out with people who acted like routinely eating at home and shopping at a local thrift store were totally normal. Plus, every time we met people from the FIRE community, we learned something new about this crazy adventure.

The retreat center was a big log cabin tucked into the woods with meeting spaces, a dining hall, and two stories of dormitory-style rooms with twin beds and shared bathrooms. Around the lodge were miles of hiking trails and a creek that boasted waterfalls and swimming holes. However, the event description made it clear that nobody was guaranteed a private room, even couples attending together. When I first told Taylor, she gave me an "over my dead body" look.

"This is the biggest Mustachian event in the world!" I told her.

"Then they won't miss me," she replied. "I'm not going to stay in the woods and share a room with people I don't know."

I promised Taylor that if we didn't get a private room, we'd sleep in the car in sleeping bags, and she reluctantly agreed. Thankfully, we didn't have to test the comfort of the CRV; we were given a cozy room on the second floor with views of the creek and the forest...and no roommate.

After settling into our room, we went to the giant meeting hall, which was packed to the brim with people. Some faces were familiar — Pete was on the deck presumably greeting old friends, and Vicki Robin was holding court with a group of awestruck fans. But most of the people were completely new to me, and they were hugging and laughing and greeting one another like long-lost friends.

"Did we bring wine?" Taylor whispered. I silently nodded. Though Taylor had agreed to come, she wasn't exactly sold on the Mr. Money Mustache ethos or even the man himself. In fact, when she first met Pete in Ecuador, she had slugged him in the chest and told him his writing was too judgy. In general, she found the Mustachian lifestyle too extreme for her taste. So how would she handle being surrounded by sixty hardcore Mustachians for an entire four days? Some people were from Seattle and Portland, but most had traveled a long distance — from Canada, Chicago, Texas, Michigan, Virginia, even Israel.

After dinner, half the group headed to bed, and the other half, Taylor and I included, headed out to the campfire. I started talking to Adrienne and Adam, a couple who were taking a "semi-retirement," which meant they had quit their jobs and were driving around the country for a year in their RV, working odd jobs for extra money. "We are trying to find the balance between having fun now and still working toward full financial independence," Adrienne explained. Across the fire, Taylor was trading stories about her years working at Microsoft with a woman who was currently working at Amazon. The woman said that her desire for financial independence wasn't about not working — she loved working — but she wanted to build her own business without putting her family at financial risk. I was so relieved that Taylor was finding people to connect with.

Lying in bed that night, Taylor and I laughed about how different our lives had become in such a short time. Not only were we voluntarily spending four days with a bunch of anticonsumerism, finance-obsessed people in the middle of the woods, but they actually felt like our people.

One of the most fascinating things about Camp Mustache was the variety of experience. Some attendees had been financially independent for years and now sheepishly admitted they didn't really talk or think about money anymore; they had come for the community. Others had just heard of FIRE and were still wrapping their minds around the idea of cutting back expenses. Some attendees who came alone said they couldn't get their spouse onboard. The standard introduction seemed to be "Hi, my name is so-and-so, and I'm about five years away from my FI date." If people mentioned their jobs, it was as an afterthought. Nobody seemed to really care what anyone else did for work.

In the first twenty-four hours, I had conversations about buying and reselling lots of land in the suburbs (*go on*), eating crickets as a renewable source of protein (*hard pass*), travel-hacking (*yes, please*), and finding an accountant who understood the quirks of FIRE (*definitely*). People talked about the struggles of feeling like the "cheap weirdo" or finding somebody to date when you're trying to save 70 percent of your income. Even though there were plenty of similarities — numerous engineers, married couples, and single men in their twenties — no two FIRE stories were alike.

Workshops covered topics like how to reach FI with kids, investing in commercial real estate, using geo-arbitrage to save on health care, and different drawdown strategies to make sure your investments are maximized. Keeping with the low-key and democratic nature of the FIRE community, each workshop was run by an attendee. There were no big presentations, no PowerPoint slides, no microphones. Just a bunch of people sitting in a circle, talking, learning, and sharing.

On the first day, I sat in on a conversation about FIRE and privilege in which Vicki Robin spoke about the enormous impact that a group of us early retirees could have on social change if we banded together. We discussed ideas like health insurance initiatives, political lobbying, and promoting financial literacy in primary school. The sessions weren't solely focused on money; I joined a session led by one of the Camp Mustache organizers, Joe, on the basics of the Wim Hof method. Wim Hof, a.k.a. "The Iceman," proved that he was able to withstand extreme cold (like climbing Mount Everest in shorts) by using breathing techniques to control his nervous system and immune system. How was this connected to financial independence? "It's about taking control of your health," one attendee mused. Another made the connection more directly: "Mustachianism is about optimizing happiness, and that's what Wim Hof is doing, too, just in a different way." It was fascinating to see the FIRE principles (invest in the things you value and skip the rest, don't worry about keeping up with the Joneses, question the status quo) applied to other parts of life, like health, wellness, and mental fortitude.

As he'd done at the party in Colorado, Pete flitted around the outskirts of conversations. Instead of inserting himself as the "guru," or standing up to welcome the campers on the first night, he was often in the back of the room, drinking a beer or chatting quietly with another Mustachian. In fact, I learned that Pete wasn't even one of the event organizers; he was an attendee who had signed up like everyone else. Watching him throughout the weekend, it occurred to me that he really was living a life of true freedom — financially and socially. He didn't seem to give a crap what anyone thought about him, and this was never more obvious than when watching him among a group of his diehard fans.

■ ■ ■ ■

The highlight of the event was the hike up Mount Si. All weekend, attendees from previous years had been talking about it. The eight-mile round-trip is frequently used as training for hikers planning to summit Mount Rainier, since the trail gains over three thousand feet in elevation in just four short miles. Depending on your fitness level, you can do this in a brisk four hours or you might be wandering home after dark. Camp Mustache even has a rule: Save a plate of food for anyone who isn't back in time for dinner.

I'd already noticed that hardiness, stoicism, and commitment are all highly valued traits in the FIRE community (and especially among Mustachians). People will joke about wearing four layers of clothing in winter, since they keep their heat so low, or about biking every day to work even in a foot of snow. Of course, for every extreme Mustachian at camp, there was another "regular" couple like us, people who live in perfectly average houses that they keep heated at a comfortable 68 degrees. However, to camp attendees, this event was more than a hike. It was a test of endurance, a chance to relish in the outdoors, and a symbol of the journey we were on: tough but rewarding.

Normally, Taylor and I would eagerly accept a physical endurance challenge, but when everyone went hiking, we chose to hang back and not go. We wanted to film a few interviews and catch up with Vicki, and we also wanted a moment to catch up with ourselves: the action at Camp Mustache had been nonstop, and we had barely had a minute alone since we arrived. This exemplified one of the changes we had been experiencing since we started this journey to financial independence. We were more willing to question activities or decisions that we would have blindly agreed to before. *Did we really want to hike a mountain, or did we want to sit peacefully in the sun together? Did we really need a brand-new stroller, or could Jovie handle another year in the one she had? Did we need our dream house, or could we settle for something more modest?* When we started, we just wanted to be more intentional with our money, but we had continued past that. We'd become more intentional with how we spent our time, who we connected to, and how we talked about our lives. This was a totally unintended, exciting change. We were becoming the people we both wanted to be.

That night, we sat around the campfire watching the hikers roll in, exhausted and sweaty. People were high-fiving and congratulating one another, sharing stories of how they had wanted to turn back but were persuaded by the rest of the group to keep going. "I'm never doing it again," one hiker said, "but

I'm glad I went." Another proudly said it was her fourth year summiting the mountain.

Now we all sat in peaceful silence around the fire. I looked around at dozens of Mustachians, old and young, men and women, all shapes and sizes. These were the people taking this journey with us. We were from all over the world, every type of person and belief system, and yet we all wanted the same thing: more moments like this.

CHAPTER 13

THE FIRE IS SPREADING

I'm writing this final chapter from my office in our house in Bend. From my window, I can see the tall thick blanket of ponderosa pine reaching toward a beautiful, sunny blue sky. The entire population of Bend is most likely outdoors today — biking or hiking or swimming or running. After I finish writing, I'll head outdoors as well, off to bike with Jovie to a nearby friend's house for a playdate.

It's August 8, 2018. One year to the day since Taylor and I drove out of San Diego for the last time, determined to find a new, simpler, freer way of life. In the past twelve months, we've given up more than half of our possessions, achieved a savings rate of over 70 percent of our income, and left our dream city for a new city. It's been a year of highs and lows. On the plus side, we've seen our net worth pass $300,000, met some of our FIRE heroes, filmed a documentary, made new friends, traveled to Ecuador, and spent precious time with our families. Yet we've also missed our Coronado friends, at times felt like weirdos with our new lifestyle, slept on couches and foldout beds for weeks on end, wondered if we've made the biggest mistake of our lives, and even been sucked back into the trap of materialism.

Last month, we shot our very last scene for the documentary. It was a bittersweet moment, full of relief and sadness. After nearly a year of being filmed, Taylor and I were getting tired of the camera. We hadn't anticipated the intrusiveness, and being subjects of the film required us to be introspective at times when we would have rather looked forward or turned off our brains completely. But the crew had also become like family. Jovie knew their names and remembered them fondly, telling us, "George made me tea," or asking, "Zippy, can we go to the park again?" At our unofficial wrap party (which is an industry tradition once the production ends), our director of photography, Ray, handed me some bacon-wrapped dates and said, "Usually if a production runs longer than a year, we are dreading the final few shoots. 'Get it over with already.' But I've always looked forward to the shoots on this film. I'm going to miss this." I looked around at the table and took everyone in. This was a family gathering, and we were going to miss our family dearly.

After withdrawing our offer on the "dream house," Taylor and I considered moving to one of the other cities on our list, but we ultimately decided Bend is where we want to live. In July, we moved into our beautiful $420,000 house. We've come to see that no "dream possession" — no home, car, or appliance — is worth more than living our dream life. Our new home is a modest 1,500-square-foot, three-bedroom place on a busy road with no backyard, but it was within our budget, is within walking distance to stores and cafés, and has a garage for our bikes and outdoor gear. FIRE is all about compromise and keeping the end goal in mind. It's asking, *Is this purchase as important as my independence?* If not, set that item back on the shelf.

Now that we've settled in Bend, we've been making new friends. Jovie has started preschool. We've adjusted to our one-car lifestyle. We've even managed to save enough money to shave another year off our FIRE date.

How far have we come? Let's recap where we were then and where we are now. In Coronado, Taylor and I were making a combined annual income of $142,000 after taxes, and our average living expenses were around $120,000.

YOU CAN RETIRE IN	**34.3 YEARS**
WITH A SAVINGS RATE OF	**16%**
ANNUAL EXPENSES	120,000
ANNUAL SAVINGS	22,000
MONTHLY EXPENSES	10,000
MONTHLY SAVINGS	1,833

If we had changed nothing, we wouldn't have reached financial independence until I was seventy-two years old and Taylor was seventy-one. Jovie would have been forty-two, probably with kids of her own.

Here is what our current lifestyle in Bend means for FIRE:

YOU CAN RETIRE IN	**10 YEARS**
WITH A SAVINGS RATE OF	**58%**
ANNUAL EXPENSES	60,000
ANNUAL SAVINGS	82,000
MONTHLY EXPENSES	5,000
MONTHLY SAVINGS	6,833

We're one year closer to FI. Taylor and I are maintaining the same level of income, and at our current savings rate, we'll be financially independent when I'm roughly forty-four and Taylor is forty-three. Jovie will be thirteen. If we maintain this, retirement will not arrive in some far-distant future; it's a goal within reach. This is empowering, and it gives us both a renewed sense of excitement to maximize our earning potential now. The better we do, the sooner we take control. Financial freedom feels close enough that I can practically taste it. As Brad Barrett from *ChooseFI* once said to me:

> Every single morning, I do realize how lucky I am to have the freedom to take my kids to the bus stop every day and to be there when they get off. To be able to sit down and do homework with them every single night. That also means I volunteer at the school all the time. I know how fortunate I am. Most middle-class suburban dads, let's say, are working forty to fifty-plus hours a week, plus a commute. My commute is to the bus stop. It's a hundred steps down the road, and that's what we do every morning. We give big hugs and we wave, and it's just this magical moment, and it's every single morning.

I can't wait to spend more free time with Jovie, and I already can see how our newfound financial cushion has reduced stress and allowed Taylor and me to be more present with our girl.

When we found FIRE, our net worth was roughly $190,000. Since then, we've seen our investments and net worth grow. We've managed to save roughly $60,000 in cash, which is what we originally expected when we budgeted our yearlong road trip. This allowed us to put a down payment on a house that we love and plan to stay in for at least a decade. There is enough left over for a healthy cushion that helps us sleep at night. It seems like the more we focus on what we value, the less we spend, so each month we save even more than the last. That is a freedom totally new to us, and we can't recommend it enough.

Further, just to clarify the numbers above and our current financial situation: Bend was easily the most expensive city on our original list (why am I not surprised?!), and we made a conscious decision to pay a little extra for the lifestyle that Bend offers, which means cutting back in other areas. Of course, we nearly lost our minds and bought a house that was way over our budget, but we caught ourselves and waited patiently for the right home to become available. Now we are paying $2,400 a month for our mortgage, which is almost exactly what we'd planned for in our original budget. When all is said and done, I estimate our annual budget will be between $50,000 and $60,000, so I used the higher estimate for the retirement calculator. We can probably spend less than $60,000, but even if we don't, that puts us comfortably at 58 percent savings rate. That's bananas! I can't express the feeling of freedom that washes over me as I look at where we were then and where we are now. This FIRE thing is potent.

We've also started asking ourselves what we want to do with our lives after FI: Taylor wants to live in Italy for a few months, learn how to play the piano, and volunteer her time at a local nursing home. I want to focus my efforts on environmental causes and start a podcast that features my dad and his friends telling old stories about their experiences in the elite special forces. Who knows, maybe I'll start a podcast about FIRE as well! We've also made a list of all the places we want to travel to, and all the new FIRE friends we want to visit. As Paula from *Afford Anything* told me:

> The thing about people who reach financial independence is that they generally tend to be very ambitious. Once you reach financial independence, you don't just stop working. You've got all this additional time that you then can spend on something that is more meaningful, whether it's creating a musical album or learning a foreign language or homeschooling your children. People who reach financial independence do all kinds of very innovative projects. I think that when you can engage in that type of innovation and creativity without having to worry about paying the bills month by month, you really are freed up to do bigger and bolder things.

As an added perk, many of our family members and friends have started to come around. For example, Chucky has reorganized his finances, has plans to pay off that new boat much sooner, and figures he has shaved ten to fifteen years off his retirement date. He recently asked me about international index fund options. We've shared our FIRE story with our close friends, and we've seen many of them join us on this path to financial independence. Even my parents have taken a more thoughtful approach to their investments and their spending. As Brad and Jonathan from *ChooseFI* like to say, "The FIRE is spreading."

■ ■ ■ ■

In many ways our story is unexceptional. Taylor and I are a fairly average middle-class American couple. We both grew up comfortably, with a fair dose of ambition and an expectation that our lives would be full of "reasonable" luxury, adventure, and success. For the most part, this has been true. What we didn't anticipate was what that luxury, adventure, and success would cost us and how paying for all that day after day would start to hold us back from actually *enjoying* our lives and having the time and freedom to *live* our lives. It's not only our happiness at stake: Continuing in our stressful and consumeristic life would have left us without the time or energy to focus on raising our daughter or on the causes we care about. Instead, we decided to make a change. We took a dramatic U-turn. We left the status quo.

For the most part, we've followed the FIRE framework pretty closely. We found cheaper housing. We got rid of our car loans and bought a less-expensive car with cash. We now cook at home far more often. We cut back on luxuries like expensive wine, gym memberships, spa appointments, and fancy gifts for others. We no longer have an endless stream of cardboard boxes delivered to our doorstep. I've met thousands of people pursuing FIRE, and they all have similar stories and have made similar life choices. The main thing that distinguishes ours is that we started by taking a yearlong journey, which we documented with a book and a film.

If you're already on the path to financial independence, you have your own story. For you, achieving FIRE may be easier or harder or look completely different. But know you are not alone. My goal with this book isn't to present our family as the model for how to achieve FIRE or as somehow "special" for making these life choices or for achieving some pinnacle of extreme frugality. We haven't! Others are much more frugal than us. In fact, my goal is the opposite: to show a fairly typical FIRE journey, one that includes all the typical anxieties, disagreements, negotiations, and mistakes that I imagine so many others would expect or even fear. I want you to see that a life of financial freedom is within reach for anyone who has the ability to live within their means — whether you're a senior vice president at Google or a barista at your local coffee shop. Whether you live in a high-cost-of-living city or the cheap countryside. You don't have to move across the country or quit your job to achieve FIRE. You don't have to do anything you don't want to do! You merely have to align what you *want* with how you *spend*. It's simple, even when it's not easy, and I hope this book serves as proof that it's possible for you.

Stumbling into the FIRE community has been one of the most rewarding experiences of my life. It's been a tough but amazing year. Even looking back at the worst times, I'm grateful to have had the chance to change my path so that I could end up here.

Today, I wonder: If we had never left Coronado, if I had never heard of Mr. Money Mustache, if I'd been unable to convince Taylor to join me in this adventure — where would I be right now? Probably stuck in a similar rut, totally burned-out by the stress of our financial burden.

This journey is about money, but it's about so much more than money. It's about finding meaning outside of work and using money as a tool — I like to picture it as a lasso — to harness that meaning in daily life. This is the beauty of FIRE: Once you see how "stuck" that luxurious, consumeristic life is, you can't unsee it. In fact, you notice it everywhere you look: the obligatory holiday parties, the roadside billboards for car financing, bumper-to-bumper commuter traffic, the new McMansion development down the road, the melancholy that sets in every Sunday evening. Likewise, once you taste a truly free life, untethered to a schedule or a paycheck or a career ladder, you can't untaste it. Once you ask yourself the most important questions — *What do I want to do with my time, and what makes me happiest?* — you can't ignore the answers.

I hope you'll consider applying the FIRE framework to your own life and feel compelled to connect with this amazing community. We're spread across the globe, moving at different paces and taking different paths, but we are all asking ourselves the same big, scary, life-changing question: How far would I go for financial freedom?

THE SEVEN STEPS TO FIRE

When I meet somebody who has just heard about FIRE and is eager to get started, they usually ask me, "What do I do first?" FIRE is summed up simply in JL Collins's manifesto "spend less that you earn — invest the surplus — avoid debt," but some of us (myself included) like to have more of a step-by-step guide. After getting the chance to meet and interview hundreds of people in the FIRE community, I compiled this list of the common steps that most people take. This is just a guide, so use what is helpful, and improve on the rest!

STEP 1: CALCULATE HOW MUCH YOU HAVE

Determine your net worth. This can be a painful exercise, but it's an absolutely vital one. Your net worth includes all your assets (cash, bank accounts, retirement funds, investments, and items of value, like houses and cars) minus all your liabilities (student loans, consumer debt, car loans, mortgages, and so on).

STEP 2: FIGURE OUT HOW MUCH YOU ARE SPENDING AND SAVING

Where is your money going? Most of us are shocked to see how much we spend on daily expenses like food and gas. I know I was. But until I knew where my money was going, I couldn't make smart changes to my spending. The key is to track. Yes, every single dollar. You can do it on paper or using an online tracker like Mint, You Need a Budget, or Personal Capital. Just make sure you're consistent, and track at least ninety days to ensure you are picking up the trends accurately. Also, start to play around with a retirement calculator. Input your current data, and then create a mock budget you think may be possible or worth working toward. Watch those mandatory working years melt away! This proved an incredibly effective incentive system for Taylor and me early on.

STEP 3: REDUCE DAILY EXPENSES

The easiest way to quickly increase your savings rate is to cut out the small stuff — cable bills, cleaning services, daily coffee purchases, phone bills, internet service, wine clubs, gym subscriptions. All these things combined can make up a significant amount of your monthly spending. Remember, this isn't about depriving yourself of what you value. It's about making choices that align with your values. Consider writing your own list of the top ten things that make you happy on a weekly basis. Another amazing tip we've picked up along the way: If you are an online shopper, leave items in your cart for three days. If you still think you need that thing three days later, perhaps you do! This has helped Taylor and me save thousands of dollars over this past year, especially during our move.

STEP 4: REDUCE THE BIG THREE: HOUSING, TRANSPORTATION, FOOD

In order to really move the dial on your savings rate, you need to tackle some big changes — things like finding a roommate, downsizing to a smaller home, buying a used car, taking public transit to work, and cooking all meals at home. Combined, these changes could increase your savings rate by 30 percent or more.

You can start small at first, but "ripping off the Band-Aid" tends to work better. That way, you don't put this off. Step 4 is scary and requires the biggest changes, which is why we don't recommend this step until you've had some time to get comfortable with your finances. Step 4 can also be the most exciting. This is your chance to reorganize your life to fit your new goals!

STEP 5: MAKE YOUR SAVINGS WORK FOR YOU

Every minute that your money is sitting in a bank account, you're missing out on the opportunity to make it work for you. Whether you're paying off high-interest debt, investing in index funds (or other funds), or buying real estate, your money should be getting the maximum return.

STEP 6: INCREASE YOUR INCOME

Many FIRE bloggers share their experiences just as we have and have found ways to earn extra money from ads, tools, or affiliate marketing links. Extra income = FIRE faster. While earning more isn't necessary, most people on the FIRE journey end up eventually focusing on growing their income in order to increase their savings rate once they've run out of expenses to cut. This may be through a traditional job, by starting a business on the side, or through picking up odd jobs to make extra cash.

STEP 7: FIND A FIRE COMMUNITY

What's the point of buying back your time if you don't have anyone to spend it with? Surrounding yourself with people on similar paths who share similar values is vital to sticking with FIRE (especially when the going gets tough). Check out the forums on *ChooseFI* and *Mr. Money Mustache*. For IRL ("in real life") meetings, there are FIRE groups in almost every region of the world.

ACKNOWLEDGMENTS

As I reflect on the lessons I've learned through this experience, one quote keeps moving to the top: "Give more, expect less." I knew very early on that I wouldn't be able to write a book, make a film, and move my family to another state without help. My wife also intuitively knew that creating personal expectations would be a dangerous game. She assured me that regardless of the outcome of this undertaking, she felt our lives were better since finding FIRE and she would love me not one ounce less if things didn't work out. After all, we could always go back to work. Plus, it turns out that the FIRE community is incredibly generous, as showcased by the countless blogs and podcasts documenting and strategizing best practices, tactics, and techniques. So, instead of focusing solely on how this project would help us, I kept an eye out for ways I could give. I sought out symbiotic relationships, with an emphasis on giving as much as we were getting. This has proved impossible. I could never sufficiently pay back the people who have contributed to this project. I am forever grateful for the love and support we've received from the onset. It speaks to the power of giving, the wonderful people I have in my life, and the FIRE community at large.

Jovie, this is all for you. I hope you will take the lessons we've shared here and use them to live your best life. I love you forever. To my beautiful, graceful, and loving wife, Taylor: You've supported me and my crazy ideas since day one. Thank you for owning this one alongside me. You are my favorite partner in the whole world. I love you. Lila and Tom Rieckens, you've fostered my creativity and always let me be me. Your constant and unwavering love has always kept me grounded. Thanks for setting the bar so high. I love you. Jan Scott, thank you for always understanding me. You are the oracle of this family and the best mother-in-law and mentor a guy could ask for. Gary Scott, I can only hope to live up to the example you've set for your daughter. Thanks for always giving us the confidence we've needed to take the big steps forward. And to Marcie, Charles, Masyn, and Ella Glenn, thanks for the enduring support that allowed us to pursue this U-turn.

Emma Pattee, your talent knows no bounds. I'll always be indebted to you for accepting this gig. You've made it so much fun, and I am damn lucky to call you a friend. Matt Brand, you set this project's course on fire and along the way showed me how to truly aim high and dream big. Ray Tsang and the entire crew at Only Today, you've been the most generous partners throughout this journey and taught me to put purpose first. And you throw a mean BBQ. Brad Barrett and Jonathan Mendonsa, you were there from the very beginning, and this project was only possible because of your undying trust, enthusiasm, support, and vision. The FIRE is spreading, my friends. Jason Gardner and everyone at New World Library, it's been an absolute pleasure. Thanks for believing in my vision and seeing it through. Here's to the next one. Travis Shakespeare, thanks for always taking the edge off. You've helped us anticipate the obstacles ahead while taking care of our story. I'm so lucky to be on this journey with you. Pete Adeney, thank you for face-punching me when I needed it the most and for never holding back. Brandon Ganch, knowing how much you value your time, I still can't believe how much of it you've donated to me. I'll happily spend a lifetime paying you back. Vicki Robin, I will never forget that perfect day on Whidbey Island, when we were awakened. Thank you for giving me the conversation of a lifetime. We won't stop here; I promise you that. Rodrigo Calderon, you showed up right when I needed you and brought this vision to life as only you could. You are as thoughtful as you are humble. They just don't make 'em like you, amigo. Marco Correia, thank you for always stepping up. You are one of the greats, my friend. I look forward to your presidency. JL Collins, thanks for writing the best book on investing and for the mentorship, laughs, and support. It's been first-class. Matt Rinkey and the team at Illumination Wealth, thank you for all the support and guidance. You exemplify professionalism in every way. Professor Stephen Berry, thanks for believing in me and sticking your neck out for me. You taught me the value of supporting others. And finally, I'm grateful to all my family and friends in Bellevue and all fellow Iowans out there. I am so lucky and proud to be a Hawkeye. Go Hawks!

ENDNOTES

Introduction to FIRE

Page 2, *Socrates tells us that the secret to happiness is found not in seeking*:
Quotes by Socrates, Confucius, and Aristotle from Chris Weller, "12
of History's Greatest Philosophers Reveal the Secret to Happiness,"
Business Insider, May 18, 2016, http://www.businessinsider.com/12
-philosophers-share-quotes-on-happiness-2016-5.

Page 2, *Even modern research shows that, to quote one study, "close relationships"*: Liz Mineo, "Good Genes Are Nice, but Joy Is Better," *Harvard
Gazette*, April 11, 2017, https://news.harvard.edu/gazette/story/2017
/04/over-nearly-80-years-harvard-study-has-been-showing-how-to
-live-a-healthy-and-happy-life.

Page 3, *Half of Americans aren't satisfied at their jobs*: Pew Research Center,
"How Americans View Their Jobs," October 6, 2016, http://www
.pewsocialtrends.org/2016/10/06/3-how-americans-view-their-jobs.

Page 5, *According to research published in* Nature, *there is an optimal point*:
Andrew T. Jebb, Louis Tay, Ed Diener, and Shigehiro Oishi, "Happiness, Income Satiation and Turning Points around the World," *Nature
Human Behavior*, January 8, 2018, https://www.nature.com/articles
/s41562-017-0277-0.

Page 7, *In 2017, consumer debt hit a record high at nearly $13 trillion*: Alan
Kline, "Slideshow: The Warning Signs in Consumer Credit Data,"
American Banker, February 11, 2018, https://www.americanbanker
.com/slideshow/the-warning-signs-in-consumer-credit-data.

Page 7, *A 2016 survey reported that 69 percent of Americans have less than*:
Niall McCarthy, "Survey: 69% Of Americans Have Less Than $1,000

In Savings [Infographic]," *Forbes*, September 23, 2016, https://www
.forbes.com/sites/niallmccarthy/2016/09/23/survey-69-of-americans
-have-less-than-1000-in-savings-infographic/#5c8e0beb1ae6.

Page 8, *A few years ago, a Wells Fargo survey found that money ranked*: Chris
Taylor, "The Last Taboo: Why Nobody Talks about Money," *Reu-
ters*, March 27, 2014, https://www.reuters.com/article/us-money
-conversation/the-last-taboo-why-nobody-talks-about-money-id
USBREA2Q1UN20140327.

Chapter 1: Work, Eat, Sleep, Repeat

Page 19, *I was curious about this episode's odd title, "Mr. Money Mustache"*:
Tim Ferriss, "Mr. Money Mustache — Living Beautifully on $25–27K
Per Year," *The Tim Ferriss Show*, February 13, 2017, https://tim.blog
/2017/02/13/mr-money-mustache.

Page 22, *The "4 percent rule," also referred to as the "safe withdrawal rate"*:
Philip L. Cooley, Carl M. Hubbard, and Daniel T. Walz, "Retirement
Savings: Choosing a Withdrawal Rate That Is Sustainable," *AAII
Journal*, February 1998, https://incomeclub.co/wp-content/uploads
/2015/04/retirement-savings-choosing-a-withdrawal-rate-that
-is-sustainable.pdf.

Chapter 2: The Million-Dollar Idea

Page 24, *a couple who retired in their thirties with three kids*: Kathleen Elkins,
"Couple That Saved $1 Million to Retire in Their 30s Share Their No.
1 Money Saving Tip," *CNBC Make It*, April 10, 2017, https://www
.cnbc.com/2017/04/10/couple-that-retired-in-their-30s-share-their
-no-1-money-saving-tip.html.

Page 25, *A man who put aside 70 percent of his IT salary*: Kathleen Elkins,
"This Couple Retired in Their 30s and Are Now Traveling Full Time
in an Airstream," *CNBC Make It*, October 19, 2017, https://www
.cnbc.com/2017/10/19/couple-retired-in-their-30s-and-are-now
-traveling-in-an-airstream.html.

Page 25, *A couple who got rid of their house and four cars*: Anna Bahney,
"This Couple Is on Track to Retire — before They Turn 40," *CNN
Money*, June 7, 2017, http://money.cnn.com/2017/06/05/retirement
/retire-early/index.html.

Page 25, *a couple who used real estate investing*: Emmie Martin, "These

30-Something School Teachers Retired with Over $1 Million after Only 8 Years of Work — Now They Travel the World," *Business Insider*, January 22, 2017, http://www.businessinsider.com/teachers-early-retirement-traveling-the-world-2017-1.

Page 28, *a blog post written by Mr. Money Mustache*: "The Shockingly Simple Math behind Early Retirement," *Mr. Money Mustache*, January 13, 2012, https://www.mrmoneymustache.com/2012/01/13/the-shockingly-simple-math-behind-early-retirement.

Chapter 3: Ten Things That Make You Happy

Page 34, *In the early years of his relationship with his wife, Jill*: Mrs. Frugalwoods, "How NOT to Pursue Financial Independence," *Frugalwoods*, January 6, 2016, https://www.frugalwoods.com/2016/01/06/how-not-to-pursue-financial-independence.

Page 38, *What really changed Taylor's thinking was an episode of the* ChooseFI *podcast*: Jonathan Mendonsa and Brad Barrett, "The Pillars of FI," *ChooseFI*, May 1, 2017, https://www.choosefi.com/021-pillars-of-fi.

Chapter 4: I Spend How Much on Coffee?!

Page 50, *To make this plan, we relied heavily on a post written by Mr. Money Mustache*: "The Shockingly Simple Math Behind Early Retirement," *Mr. Money Mustache*, January 13, 2012, https://www.mrmoneymustache.com/2012/01/13/the-shockingly-simple-math-behind-early-retirement.

Page 55, *The* Frugalwoods *family wrote that they paid to eat out only two times a year*: Mrs. Frugalwoods, "How We Broke Our Eating Out Habit in 9 Steps," *Frugalwoods*, July 6, 2015, https://www.frugalwoods.com/2015/07/06/how-we-broke-our-eating-out-habit-in-9-steps.

Page 55, *Brad from the* ChooseFI *podcast mentioned*: Jonathan Mendonsa and Brad Barrett, "Friday Roundup: Paul Case Study Part 4," *ChooseFI*, June 2, 2017, https://www.choosefi.com/025r-friday-roundup-paul-case-study-part-4.

Page 55, *And Pete from* Mr. Money Mustache *continually espoused*: "Is a Costco Membership Worth the Price?," *Mr. Money Mustache*,

September 30, 2011, https://www.mrmoneymustache.com/2011
/09/30/is-a-costco-membership-worth-the-cost.

Page 56, *I used the "Latte Factor Calculator" created by Financial Mentor*:
"Latte Factor Calculator," *Financial Mentor*, accessed August 29,
2018, https://financialmentor.com/calculator/latte-factor-calculator.

Chapter 5: BMWs and Boat Clubs

Page 62, *Economists call this the "sunk cost fallacy"*: "Sunk Cost Fallacy,"
behavioraleconomics.com, accessed August 29, 2018, https://www
.behavioraleconomics.com/resources/mini-encyclopedia-of-be
/sunk-cost-fallacy.

Page 68, *As Mr. Money Mustache points out in his article "Top 10 Cars"*:
"Top 10 Cars for Smart People," *Mr. Money Mustache*, March 19,
2012, https://www.mrmoneymustache.com/2012/03/19/top
-10-cars-for-smart-people.

Chapter 6: Goodbye, Coronado

Page 78, *a thread on Reddit titled "Documentaries relevant to FIRE"*: "Documentaries Relevant to FIRE," *Reddit* (r/financial independence),
accessed August 29, 2018, https://www.reddit.com/r/financial
independence/comments/80a2p7/documentaries_relevant_to_fire.

Page 78, Mr. Money Mustache *had reached more than twenty-three million
people*: Tim Ferriss, "Mr. Mustache — Living Beautifully on $25–27K
Per Year," *The Tim Ferriss Show*, accessed August 29, 2018,
https://tim.blog/2017/02/13/mr-money-mustache.

Page 78, *there are nearly 400,000 people on the Financial Independence
subreddit*: "Initial Financial Independence Survey Results Are Here!,"
Reddit (r/financial independence), accessed August 29, 2018,
https://www.reddit.com/r/financialindependence.

Page 85, *Amazingly enough, they mentioned the documentary project*:
Jonathan Mendonsa and Brad Barrett, "Friday Roundup: Paul Case
Study Part 4," *ChooseFI*, June 9, 2017, https://www.choosefi.com
/026r-friday-roundup.

Chapter 7: The Journey Begins

Page 94, *Geo-arbitrage, a term made popular by Tim Ferriss*: "Introduction
to Geoarbitarge," *Alt Lifehack*, June 15, 2009, https://altlifehack
.wordpress.com/2009/06/15/introduction-to-geoarbitrage.

Chapter 8: What the Heck Is an Index Fund?

Page 110, *JL has a "Stock Series"*: JL Collins, "Stock Series" (The Simple Path to Wealth), *jlcollinsnh*, accessed August 29, 2018, http://jlcollinsnh.com/stock-series.

Page 112, *When he was recently asked how he would invest his first million dollars*: Tim Ferriss, "Picking Warren Buffett's Brain: Notes from a Novice, *The Tim Ferriss Show*, accessed August 29, 2018, https://tim.blog/2008/06/11/061108-picking-warren-buffetts-brain-notes-from-a-novice.

Page 112, *In his 2014 bestseller* Money: Master the Game, *Tony Robbins describes how:* Tony Robbins, *Money: Master the Game* (New York: Simon & Schuster, 2014), 488–89.

Page 114, *Then I heard Brad Barrett of the* ChooseFI *podcast*: Jonathan Mendonsa and Brad Barrett, "Let's Talk about Fees: Why Investment Fees Are Evil and How to Avoid Them," *ChooseFI*, December 23, 2016, https://www.choosefi.com/003-investment-fees-evil-avoid.

Chapter 9: Getting Schooled in FIRE

Page 124, *FinCon, one of the largest personal finance media conferences in the world*: "Over 1,500 Personal Finance Experts and Enthusiasts to Gather at FinCon, 'the Comic-Con of Money,' in Dallas This October," *PRLeap*, October 10, 2017, http://www.prleap.com/pr/258254/over-1500-personal-finance-experts-and.

Page 127, *we were in an unprecedentedly strong and long-lasting bull market*: Michael Santoli, "Second Longest Bull Market Ever Aging Gracefully but Investors Wonder How Long It Will Last," *CNBC*, September 13, 2017, https://www.cnbc.com/2017/09/13/second-longest-bull-market-ever-aging-gracefully-but-investors-wonder-how-long-it-will-last.html.

Page 129, *One of the most popular techniques is a Roth conversion ladder*: "How to Access Retirement Funds Early," *Mad Fientist*, accessed August 29, 2018, https://www.madfientist.com/how-to-access-retirement-funds-early.

Page 131, *Using the free "Buy vs. Rent" calculator offered by the* New York Times: Mike Bostock, Shan Carter, and Archie Tse, "Is It Better to Rent or Buy?," *New York Times* (The Upshot), accessed August 29, 2018, https://www.nytimes.com/interactive/2014/upshot/buy-rent-calculator.html.

Chapter 10: Family and Frugality

Page 145, *I had read an article called "Financially Independent Retired Early"*: Steve, "Financially Independent Retired Early: Flaws with Philosophy?," *Evergreen Small Business*, July 23, 2017, https://evergreensmallbusiness.com/financially-independent-retired-early-flaws.

Page 149, *Pete from* Mr. Money Mustache *also makes this point*: "Happiness Is the Only Logical Pursuit, *Mr. Money Mustache*, June 8, 2016, https://www.mrmoneymustache.com/2016/06/08/happiness-is-the-only-logical-pursuit.

Chapter 11: Dream House or Dream Life?

Page 156, *I read a* Washington Post *article about Bend*: Nathan Borchelt, "Bend, Ore., a City You'll Love to Hate," *Washington Post* (Travel), October 12, 2012, https://www.washingtonpost.com/lifestyle/travel/bend-ore-the-city-youll-love-to-hate/2012/10/04/9a7e2f10-042e-11e2-91e7-2962c74e7738_story.html.

Page 163, *Then I remembered an interview with financial expert Michael Kitces*: "Michael Kitces — The 4% Rule and Financial Planning for Early Retirement," *Mad Fientist*, accessed August 29, 2018, https://www.madfientist.com/michael-kitces-interview.

Chapter 12: Finding Our FIRE Friends

Page 168, *our trip coincided with the island's heaviest rainfall in recorded history*: John Hopewell, "Historic Rain Inundates Kauai, Cutting Off Hawaii Residents and Tourists with Floods and Mudslides," *Washington Post*, April 17, 2018, https://www.washingtonpost.com/news/capital-weather-gang/wp/2018/04/17/historic-rain-inundates-kauai-cutting-off-hawaii-tourists-with-floods-and-mudslides/?utm_term=.919bea8b7e83.

Page 173, *Wim Hof, a.k.a. "The Iceman," proved*: "Learn Everything You Need to Know about the Wim Hof Method," *Wim Hof Method*, accessed August 29, 2018, https://www.wimhofmethod.com.

Page 174, *The eight-mile round-trip is frequently used as training for hikers planning*: Christy Karras, "A First-Timer's Primer for Hiking Mount Si without Tears," *Seattle Times* (Travel), September 14, 2016, https://www.seattletimes.com/life/travel/a-first-timers-primer-for-hiking-mount-si-without-tears.

INDEX

release date, 6; video production crew for, 97; wrap party for, 179

playingwithfire.co, 25

possessions: happiness and, 2; meaning of, in our lives, 67; unused, 84–85

prescription drugs, 52

privilege, 125, 183

public transportation, 188

Quito (Ecuador), 120

rationalizations, 162

real estate investments, 19, 189

Reddit, 78

Reno (NV), 14

rental income, 46, 127

renting vs. homeownership, 131

retirement: calculator for, 39–41, 65–66, 180; as goal, 95; lost-wages flaw and, 149–50; mini-retirements, 46; working after, 133–34

retirement accounts, 16, 102, 129

retirement calculator, 39–41, 65–66, 180

Rich & Regular (blog), 25

Rieckens, Jovie: birth of, 15, 60; childcare for, 16, 74

Rieckens, Scott: boat club membership of, 61–62, 67, 74; documentary films of, 78; "dream life" focus of, 13–14, 90–91; economic background of, 183; introduction to FIRE, 19–21; job dissatisfaction of, 24, 78–79; marriage/honeymoon of, 13–14; personal mission statement of, 151–52; as salaried worker, 17–18, 24;

San Diego–area home search of, 74–78, 160, 162; as video production company officer, 14–15, 17, 79; yearlong trip of, 81–82, 83, 126–27, 181

Rieckens, Taylor: and author's persuasive attempts with FIRE, 27–29, 30–31, 34–42; "BMW saga" of, 60–61, 64–67, 74, 144; "dream life" focus of, 13–14, 90–91; economic background of, 183; employment of, 14, 81, 160–61; marriage/honeymoon of, 13–14; Mustachians and, 171; San Diego–area home search of, 74–78. *See also* Taylor's Takes

risk taking, 166

Robbins, Tony, 112

Robin, Vicki, 64, 78, 97–100, 171, 173, 175

Roth, J.D., 125, 151–52

Roth conversion ladder, 129

Sabatier, Grant, 125

San Diego (CA), 12, 14–15. *See also* Coronado (CA)

Saunders, Julien, 25

Saunders, Kiersten, 25

savings: author's experience, 10; average household, 7; focus on, 102; income increases for, 189; investing, 3, 189; investments vs., 126; retirement calculator using, 39–41; tracking, 188

Seattle (WA), 137, 142; author's stay in, 91–95, 106, 108; in author's travel plan, 83, 90; FIRE community members in/near, 96–100

"semi-retirement," 171

INDEX

207

ABOUT THE
AUTHOR

Scott Rieckens is an Emmy-nominated film/video producer, serial entrepreneur, and author. Scott has spent his career as a storyteller connecting people with ideas. Along the way, his work has generated millions of views through a feature-length documentary, multiple television series, short films, and a diverse range of commercial projects for Microsoft, NBC, Facebook, FOX, Taylor Guitars, WIRED, and others. Scott's latest endeavor, *Playing with FIRE*, explores the growing community of frugal-minded folks choosing a path to financial independence and early retirement. He and his family reside in Bend, Oregon.

playingwithfire.co